CH

D0429015

THE DOZIER SCHOOL FOR BOYS

Forensics, Survivors, and a Painful Past

ELIZABETH A. MURRAY, PhD

TWENTY-FIRST CENTURY BOOKS / MINNEAPOLIS

This book was written to honor and support all who suffered at the Dozier School for Boys, including those who came forth to tell their stories and those who could not. It is my hope that in relating the accounts of the men of Dozier, I can help convey the power of abuse and the power of truth telling. Although reading the heartbreaking accounts of the Dozier survivors is difficult, it was an honor to write this story and promote their cause. I hope they someday find peace and justice. I also dedicate this book to my grandson, Sam; may he grow to be wise and strong and work to promote justice and healing.

My sincere appreciation goes to my four-time editor, Domenica Di Piazza. She sure has a way with my words! I am also grateful to all the fellow authors who have written about Dozier, from the survivors to the journalists, especially Carol Marbin Miller, who took the lead from the outset and made things happen.

Text copyright © 2020 by Elizabeth A. Murray

Twenty-First Century Books™
An imprint of Lerner Publishing Group, Inc.
241 First Avenue North
Minneapolis, MN 55401 USA

For reading levels and more information, look up this title at www.lernerbooks.com.

Main body text set in Adobe Garamond Pro Regular.
Typeface provided by Adobe Systems.

Library of Congress Cataloging-in-Publication Data

The Cataloging-in-Publication Data for *The Dozier School for Boys: Forensics, Survivors, and a Painful Past* is on file at the Library of Congress.
ISBN 978-1-5415-1978-7 (lib. bdg.)
ISBN 978-1-5415-6269-1 (eb pdf)

Manufactured in the United States of America
1-44314-34560-2/25/2019

Contents

The Dozier School was founded to house troubled and lawbreaking youth. Its goals were to help them learn skills and build character before being released back into society. From the outside, the school appeared to be a cheerful environment, as in this 1957 photo of boys arriving at Dozier by bus. But the school held dark secrets of abuse and suffering.

Chapter I
REFORMING WAYWARD YOUTH

The fire began on the ground floor of the Florida State Reform School dormitory in the early hours of the morning. When the fire was first discovered at three thirty, about one hundred boys and several employees were asleep in their beds on the third floor of the building. When the night watchman's calls awakened them, they realized they were trapped. The upstairs fire escape doors were locked, and flames blocked the main stairway. The building's wooden floors had recently been painted with oil-based paint and were burning rapidly. The residents scrambled frantically to get out. Many ran to an alternate stairwell and escaped. Others were not so fortunate. One boy and two employees near the fire escape fell to their deaths through the collapsing floor. Others died elsewhere in the building, most likely from smoke inhalation. The dormitory burned completely to the ground. The charred remains of several bodies were recovered from the fire's residue and were buried in Boot Hill, the school cemetery. The cause of the fire and the number of dead were never confirmed and are still debated.

"CHARACTER FITTING FOR A GOOD CITIZEN"

The Florida State Reform School was a juvenile incarceration center established by Florida law in 1897. Located near the town of Marianna in Jackson County, the school's mission was to be an institution that was "not simply a place of correction, but a reform school, where the young offender of the law, separated from vicious associates, may receive careful physical, intellectual, and moral training, be reformed and restored to the community with purposes and character fitting for a good citizen, an honorable and honest man, with a trade or skilled occupation fitting such person for self-maintenance."

By 1914, the year of the fire at the school, the United States was a prosperous nation. The Industrial Revolution of the previous century had brought machine-based manufacturing to Europe and the United States. The new technologies were mechanized and powered by steam-based, coal-powered engines. Transportation, communication, and farming industries no longer solely relied on animal and human hand labor. They were becoming more reliant on machines built by workers in factories.

Thousands of Americans migrated to cities, hoping for jobs in the factories. But instead of prosperity, many found poverty and despair. Without labor laws to protect them, children worked twelve- to sixteen-hour shifts in factories for only one or two dollars a day. And because they were small, children also worked in narrow, underground mine shafts, digging up coal to power the engines of steam locomotives and factories, and to heat homes and other buildings. Women, too, worked long hours in factories for little pay. Men often worked into old age because Social Security and other financial support for retirement did not yet exist. Nonetheless, most Americans believed that a strong work ethic was the key to success. They held to an old saying that "idle hands are the devil's workshop."

At this same time in US history, ideas about education, criminal justice, and civil rights were shifting. New theories in the fields of psychology and sociology were beginning to influence family life and public institutions, including the legal system. Reformatory schools came out of these new ideas. The schools were places to house juvenile offenders. Before this time, juveniles and adult criminals served their sentences together. At the reform schools, youth would receive an education and training in the technological skills needed for the new manufacturing era. Also known as industrial schools, reformatory schools began to emerge throughout the United States to house and reform delinquent children.

ESTABLISHING ORDER

The Florida State Reform School opened its doors on January 1, 1900. It was originally set on 1,200 acres (486 ha) in northwestern Florida and later grew to 1,400 acres (567 ha). At one point, it was the largest reform school for youth in the United States—too large to be fenced in. The school's original main building was beautiful and white. It sat on a hill, nestled in farmland and approached by a lovely tree-lined road. Workers put up additional buildings over time, including dormitories and dining facilities.

According to the law, residents of the schools were to be boys and girls under the age of sixteen who had been convicted of crimes, either felonies or misdemeanors (less serious wrongdoings). The children could be sentenced to the reformatory for not less than six months

The Dozier School was a segregated institution for much of its history. Black inmates lived and worked separately from white inmates. These black students are eating a meal, supervised by staff, at the school's dining hall in the mid-twentieth century.

and not more than four years. In addition, any court in Florida could commit children who were "incorrigible" (uncontrollable) or who engaged in "vicious conduct" to the school for guardianship, as long as they were between the ages of ten and sixteen.

From the beginning, the school was segregated by race. The law said, "There shall be two separate buildings, not nearer than one-fourth mile [0.4 km] to each other, one for white and one for negroes . . . white and negro convicts shall not be, in any manner, associated together or worked together." The southern portion of the campus housed whites. The northern area held what people at the time called "colored" students. The school remained segregated until 1968. From its first year, and throughout much of its history, the majority of residents were nonwhite. In 1900 thirty students attended the school, but only five were white (all boys). The other twenty-five children were "colored" boys and girls.

Reforming Wayward Youth

Race Vocabulary

The vocabulary of race has changed over time in the United States. In the early twentieth century, the words *colored* and *negro* were commonly used to refer to black people. Historians who study the Florida reform school therefore assume that in documents where the term *colored* is used, it refers to black students. From photographs, historians can also tell that black youth made up the majority of nonwhite students at the school. However, later records from the school include first and last names of Hispanic origin. Historians do not know exactly how school leaders decided in which category to place each child. This book will use the word *black* for the people the school viewed as "colored." Florida's cultural history is rich and varied, so it is possible that individuals at the school also included people of European as well as Cuban and other Caribbean heritage, American Indians (sometimes called Native Americans), and possibly people of Asian heritage.

The law allowed the state's governor to appoint five people to oversee the school. These five commissioners would report every two years to the state legislature about the institution's progress and condition. The commissioners did not receive a salary. They were paid only for their personal expenses while fulfilling their duties. Each county that sent a child to the school had to pay $50 per year per student to cover food, lodging, and clothing. When the school became self-sustaining through the children's labor, the fee would be dropped.

The school's superintendent received a maximum salary of $600 per year. The assistant superintendent received no more than $400 per year. Two female staff members, known as matrons, earned no more than $300 per year. The superintendent could hire a physician, as needed, for a sum not to exceed $300 per year, "to render medical aid and assistance in all cases of sickness or diseases" to the youth at the school.

The school was set up to be self-sufficient. Residents and employees were to grow their own food, cook their own meals, wash clothes and bedding, manufacture the school's furniture, and repair its equipment. At first, the school didn't have enough inmates to do all the work. To increase the number of inmates, the school asked Florida's governor to allow authorities to send any unruly child, even those without a court conviction, to the school. The school also asked that its leaders—not a court—set the length of the child's sentence. And the school also requested that it be allowed to keep inmates past the age of eighteen, if school officials thought it necessary. Florida lawmakers agreed. By 1905 the laws governing the school had been updated, and the school's population grew.

Under the laws, children at the school would be "disciplined, instructed, employed, and governed." The commissioners set the guidelines for the school, and the staff were to carry out the rules, including those for education and punishments. The state law gave no specifics for how the children would be educated, other than in "branches of useful knowledge adapted to their age and capacity." They would receive instruction in mechanical trades and agricultural pursuits, "according to their ages, strength, disposition, and capacity; and otherwise as will best secure their reformation, amendment and future benefit." In their management of the school, the commissioners were to set up specific guidelines, including for punishments. They could fire employees who did not carry out their orders.

Officials had the right to remove residents of the school who misbehaved or tried to escape and send them to jail or state prison. If thrown out of the school, the person had to serve the entire original sentence. Their time already spent at the school was not counted toward the sentence. No juvenile offender who was blind, deaf, mute, or "insane" (the term for mental illness at the time) would be sent to the institution. The school could also refuse any child offender if that person was thought to be too difficult to manage.

"NOTHING TO REFORM; MUCH TO DEGRADE"

The Florida State Reform School was meant to be a place of training, education, and rehabilitation for young offenders. Yet, shortly after the school opened, inspectors reported serious problems with the care provided to residents. A 1903 inspection found children as young as six chained in leg restraints. A report from 1909 found not a single desk in the school building. Two years later, the 1911 report revealed sickness, overcrowding, and hunger. The report also pointed to accounts of adult staff hitting inmates with a leather strap as punishment. And in 1914, the dormitory burned to the ground, killing six boys (or seven—the number was never determined exactly) and two adult staff. The school's main office was in the dormitory, and fourteen years of records were destroyed in the fire.

At the time of the fire, the superintendent was a young man who was said to be hardly old enough to hold the position. He had gone into the town of Marianna that night for entertainment with three other school employees. The investigation of the fire concluded that if the men had been at the school that night, the tragedy might not have happened. The superintendent was therefore fired. The school rebuilt its housing for white students, choosing smaller cottages for fewer inmates so that escape in case of fire would be easier. Black students remained in a large building without fire escapes.

On April 9, 1915, a newspaper article titled "Reform School Needs Reformation" brought more light to major problems at the school. The article stated that former students, both girls and boys, had reported being raped by school employees. Some had contracted "incurable and filthy diseases," probably referring to sexually transmitted infections. Boys claimed they had been sent to work at private farms rather than working at the school as they were meant to do. The article also described the school and its residents, noting that "they are improperly clothed; taught almost nothing; that filth and ignorance prevails; that for a long time the institution has done practically nothing to reform; much to degrade." The article concluded with pointed criticism of the school. "It has been a juvenile convict camp, with worse treatment for the inmates than has been given adult convicts in this state for 20 years."

THE FLU EPIDEMIC

In addition to other diseases, the 1918 worldwide outbreak of Spanish influenza struck the school and neighboring areas. Globally, the outbreak lasted nearly two years. About 500 million people, or one-third of the world's population at the time, were infected. At least 50 million people died, and about 675,000 of those deaths were in the United States. In October 1918, around 50 percent of Florida residents in Jackson County caught the flu virus. The school, which by then had been renamed the Florida Industrial School for Boys, was hit much harder. The flu spread rapidly at the school. Records indicate that almost 99 percent (264 of 267) of its students came down with the virus at the same time. Conditions at the school deteriorated quickly. For example, when the school's engineer and his student staff came down with the flu, they were too weak to get out of bed to manage the power system. So the school lost lighting and the power to run its water pumps. Without working pumps, the school had limited water and could not remove its sewage.

Streetcar conductors in New York City wear face masks to protect against the Spanish flu in 1918. The epidemic hit Dozier too. Nearly all inmates became sick with the flu, and eleven boys died.

Reforming Wayward Youth

The first person to die of the flu at the school was a black female employee. Staff members were so sick they could not immediately prepare her grave, and she was not buried for nearly a day. The Spanish flu also took the lives of eleven boys at the school. A doctor who visited the school during the outbreak reported gruesome conditions there. By 1919 public outcry demanded the school be shut down until it could be brought up to safer conditions.

By 1921 much-needed changes were falling into place at the school. For example, the school had seven teachers leading elementary and high school classes. Some students were learning about farming and various industries, while others were receiving military training. Plans were also underway to construct at least fifteen new buildings. As one historian noted, the school "is rapidly becoming what it was intended to be—a real reclamation school for delinquent boys."

ANYTHING BUT HONORABLE

By the mid-1920s, the school's population had grown from about 250 to around 300 students. This was twice the number for which the school had originally been built, so overcrowding was again a problem. Mistreatment of students had resumed as well. In 1926 an inspection again found children restrained with chains on their ankles. In 1941 one boy's mother publicly accused the school of abuse. She reported that school officials had beaten her son bloody with a wooden board that was 3 inches (7.6 cm) thick. School officials countered that the boy had earned the beating, which they described as a spanking only. The superintendent also responded to the allegation of abuse by having the governor of Florida—a former schoolteacher—provide a personal endorsement for school paddling as an acceptable form of discipline.

Around this same time, a young employee at the school named Arthur G. Dozier was moving up the ranks. Born in 1910, Dozier had begun his long career at the school in 1934 as a teacher. He briefly served as the director for the black students before being named

Dozier by Any Other Name

The Arthur G. Dozier School for Boys had various official names throughout its history. It began in 1900 as the Florida State Reform School and in 1914 was renamed the Florida Industrial School for Boys. In 1957 the institution became the Florida School for Boys. It was called the Arthur G. Dozier School for Boys from 1968 until its closing in 2011. Regardless of the actual name by which the school was known at any point in time, for convenience and clarity this book will refer to the institution as the Dozier School or simply as Dozier.

director of the white campus in 1941. During World War II (which lasted from 1939 to 1945), Dozier left the school for three years to serve in the US Army. He returned to the school after the war and became its superintendent in 1946.

Under Dozier's supervision, the population at the school at one point swelled to about nine hundred students. The school hired more staff but not enough to govern, care for, or teach that many boys. Accounts surfaced of violence among the students and between employees and boys. So did stories of frequent attempts to escape. There were even tales of boys who simply disappeared, with allegations that staff had beaten or worked them to death.

Dozier left the school in 1957. That same year, the facility changed its name to the Florida School for Boys. Following Dozier's death in 1967, the institution was again renamed—the Arthur G. Dozier School for Boys—to honor the former superintendent. Many people would come to report, however, that Superintendent Arthur Dozier was anything but honorable. The same was said of many of his employees. Thousands of children were sentenced to the institution during its 111-year lifetime (1900–2011). Some inmates survived to give firsthand reports of the horrors they endured at the hands of those whose job it was to care for them. The fates of most of the others will never be known.

Dozier residents did the work to keep the school campus well groomed and beautiful. This undated image shows the school's dormitory buildings.

Chapter 2
SUNUP TO SUNDOWN

Inmate Johnny Lee Gaddy saw a boy on Dozier's logging crew lose his hand to a chain saw. On another occasion, he saw a human hand in the school's trash pit. Students at Dozier warned incoming boys about the "shake" and the "feel." As a form of hazing, a resident boy would shake his bare genitals against a new and unsuspecting boy. Or he might try to feel another boy's private parts in the shower or at night. Teachers threw tennis balls at any boy who fell asleep in class. If a boy ran away to escape humiliation or violence at the school, the boys he left behind were punished. He, too, would be brutally punished if school officials caught him.

Yet from the outside, Dozier School looked charming. Numerous accounts describe the school's beautiful grounds and lovely buildings. Lawns and shrubs were manicured with care. Attractive plantings adorned the walkways and drives. The floors, woodwork, and furniture inside the buildings showed great attention to detail and were crafted with skill, some of it by Dozier boys themselves.

The campus had at least one hundred different buildings. In addition to administrative offices, cottages, dining facilities, and schoolhouses, the school had recreational spaces, clinics, and a variety of workshops. And because the school was segregated, each campus had its own similar structures. For example, each campus had an identical chapel to ensure that black and white students did not worship together.

ARRIVING AT DOZIER SCHOOL

Historians are piecing together the story of life at Dozier School from written historical records. They also have some firsthand accounts of daily life at the school from boys, now men, who have described their days there. These sources tell the story of life at Dozier during the 1950s, 1960s, and 1970s. During that period, Dozier School accepted boys between eleven and seventeen years old from all counties in Florida. Boys usually arrived by bus or police car. Staff registered them in the main office. They gave incoming boys booklets about the expectations and rules at the school, even though many of them could not read. The boys were assigned an identity number and received a haircut, a medical exam, and any necessary vaccinations. Staff either assigned newcomers to a temporary dorm for new students or to a cottage with boys of the same age.

Boys who were sentenced to Dozier not only went to school there; they also worked for the benefit of the school and the State of Florida. So each incoming boy got an initial job assignment for which he received work clothes. He also met with staff at the guidance center for a psychological evaluation. A new boy underwent academic testing and received a school uniform.

A new arrival at Dozier in the 1950s receives work clothes from Superintendent Arthur Dozier, for whom the school was named.

SUPERVISORS, STAFF, AND STUDENTS

By the 1950s, the school staff consisted of approximately 150 personnel, mostly men. They were supervisors of staff and students, teachers, coaches, maintenance crew, and clinicians for medical and psychological consultations. Most of the employees were white. Some were black. Many had college degrees. Some had served in the military or had worked in prisons. Some of the staff came from the nearby town of Marianna. Most lived on site at the school.

At the start of 1958, 761 boys lived on campus. A little more than half—423 boys—were white, and the other 338 were listed as "colored." Housing was racially segregated. Cottages on the white side of the property were named for US presidents such as Abraham Lincoln and Grover Cleveland. On the black side of campus, they were named for "outstanding Negro leaders" such as baseball player Jackie Robinson and boxer Joe Louis. The campus had nineteen two-story cottages, each home to about forty boys. In the cottages, the boys slept in a large, open room on the first floor, either in bunk beds or in army-style single cots. The boys had no privacy in their sleeping quarters or bathrooms.

Adults lived with the boys and were called cottage fathers, or house parents if they were a married couple living on campus. Cottage fathers usually had separate quarters upstairs. If a dorm had two cottage fathers, the one on duty slept downstairs with the boys. If a dorm had only one cottage father, he went upstairs after the boys were in bed. Night watchmen walked the grounds and went into the buildings to make sure all boys were in bed. The lights were never fully turned out.

New students quickly found someone, maybe a boy from their hometown, who was willing to help them learn the ins and outs of campus life. They would warn the newcomers how to stay out of trouble with the cottage fathers and the instructors. They would point out the boys who stole from others. They would warn new boys about the peer abuses called the "shake" and the "feel." Tension was constant between kids who looked for trouble and those who tried to avoid it.

Some boys were models of positive peer pressure. If they helped steer others away from problems and kept peace in their cottages, they moved up the ranks and earned more benefits. The school had six ranks of achievement, based on behavior. Boys could advance from grub, rookie, and explorer, to pioneer, pilot, and ace. Boys were rookies when they first arrived at the school. Grub was a demotion from any rank. Ranks determined privileges. For example, grubs were not allowed to watch TV. Pioneers were allowed to go into the nearby town of Marianna on alternate weeks for a movie or to the skating rink. Pilots had all the privileges of pioneers and could also go to the home games of the local high school sports teams. They were also allowed to write one extra letter home each week. Aces could go to Marianna for a half day each week, unescorted, and could write unlimited letters home. No boy was allowed off the school's campus until he had reached at least the rank of pioneer. No more than four or five boys at the school held the ace rank at any given time.

Boys earned promotions if they were able to keep peace in their cottages. But fights did break out, sometimes resulting in "putting a lamp out" (giving another kid a black eye with one punch), "going to duke city" (getting into a full-blown fistfight), or "turning the cottage out" (a public fight among several boys). Cottage fathers sometimes supervised boxing matches between two boys who couldn't get along. Boys who got into full-on fistfights got a write-up, known as a "grade." The write-up led to a demotion in rank and sometimes to a far more severe punishment.

RISE AND SHINE

Each day at the Dozier School started around six in the morning with a bugle call and flag ceremony. Boys with responsibilities such as milking cows or preparing breakfast in the dining hall got up earlier. Boys had less than ten minutes to make their beds, shower, and dress for their day of work or school. Showers were timed. The boys would then line up to march together from their cottage to the dining hall, about one-quarter of a mile (0.4 km) away. Work and school began at quarter to eight.

At the end of each day, the boys also marched together, by cottage, to the cafeteria for dinner. Then they returned to their cottages and did cleaning or yard work around their dormitory. Students were expected to shine their shoes or boots each night. They were also responsible for taking care of their clothes. If a button came off, they had to sew it back on. If an item was torn, they had to fix it. If any time remained, boys with privileges might be able to watch television in their cottage. Lights-out was no later than ten, and earlier for boys who had early-morning duties.

Dozier boys had classes or work five and a half days a week, with half days of school or work on Saturday. During the rest of the weekend, boys could watch TV, play Ping-Pong, or play cards or dominoes. They could participate in sports too. Each cottage had a basketball hoop and sports teams, and the campus had pits for playing horseshoes. Dozier's intramural teams were arranged by cottages, whose boys competed against one another. The school's varsity teams

Residents at Dozier had little free time. When their chores were done, boys who had earned good-conduct privileges were allowed to relax. This undated photo, likely from the 1940s, shows students listening to the radio. In later decades, the dormitories had televisions.

were segregated and competed against public schools in the area, which were also segregated. The two campuses, black and white, held talent shows and holiday pageants. They also had bands that played at campus sporting events or in local off-campus parades. Yet any fun or friendship was temporary and short-lived. The school wasn't home, and most boys who had families missed them deeply.

BOYS AT WORK

As an industrial school, Dozier expected boys to work one day and go to school the next. The school had an even- and odd-day system. In other words, each day some boys went to school, while others worked. The next day, the groups traded places. Workdays lasted a full eight hours. School days went until mid-afternoon, followed by organized recess activities until dinnertime.

Dozier had a large working farm and dairy to provide food for

Black students performed most of the agricultural work and care of livestock at Dozier, including the school's dairy cows, as shown in this photo from the 1950s.

the school. The school sold some of the food to help pay for running the facility. Goods that the boys manufactured at the school were also sold to the public. From videos and personal accounts, historians know that white boys at Dozier learned trades such as electronics, printing, machining, automotive mechanics, and woodworking. Black boys did much of the school's general construction, agricultural work, meat production, and dairy labor.

Black students also fed and tended the school's resident animals, which included chickens, pigs, dairy cows, beef cattle, and an occasional bull. Mules had been at the school, but by the late 1950s, work animals had largely been replaced by heavy machinery. Chickens provided eggs and meat for Sunday dinners. The cows yielded milk that was turned into a variety of dairy products. Dozier had milking machines and even relied on artificial insemination to impregnate female cows. Boys on the dairy crew milked cows once around four in the morning and then again at two in the afternoon. Those with early-morning duties were often grouped in the same cottages so that boys who worked the dairy or cooked breakfast wouldn't disturb others.

Black students were also the ones to slaughter livestock. They plucked the chickens, butchered the animal carcasses, and processed the meat into bacon, ham, and sausage. Some students collected food scraps from the campus dining halls and recycled them into slop to feed the pigs. This work instilled terror in the boys. For example, when former student Johnny Lee Gaddy had this job, he says he saw a human foot in the hog "slop pot" and once saw a hand in the trash pit. Gaddy and other Dozier survivors believe that Dozier staff executed some boys and disposed of their body parts by feeding them to the pigs. Other former students suspect that fellow inmates either died while doing dangerous work or were killed while trying to escape and that staff dumped their bodies into the swamp. Either way, boys disappeared from Dozier without explanation.

Much of the work the boys did—especially the black students—was little more than slave labor. Some people claimed that the school hired out teams of black students as field laborers to work at private, off-campus farms. The farms paid the school for the work, but the boys themselves received no money for their labor. The school claimed it was simply fulfilling its mission to give the boys usable skills. It was also committed to saving the State of Florida money by making the school self-sufficient, producing as much of its own food and furnishings as possible.

Documents from the time reveal that Dozier boys could choose their work assignments based on their interests. School officials placed incoming boys in work crews. They might take a boy's previous experience or skills into consideration. If the student had none, supervisors would place the boy with lawn and landscape or food service teams as a starting point. Food service workers had a broad range of low-skill responsibilities, from setup and cleanup to serving or cooking. The landscape crew was a helpful place for a boy to learn his way around campus quickly.

Sunup to Sundown

Practical work that would help boys find employment after their release from Dozier included jobs in the sewing, shoe repair, and upholstery shops. Some boys also learned barbering at one of the two campus barbershops, one for blacks and one for whites. Other students learned clerical skills such as typing and filing paperwork in the various offices on campus. Some learned basic medical duties and assisted in the institution's hospital.

Boys needed some level of training before joining skilled maintenance teams, which included carpentry, construction, painting, woodwork, electrical, plumbing, and mechanics. Boys at the school's auto mechanics division repaired and maintained all the vehicles on campus. These included cars and trucks as well as the heavy equipment for agricultural work. The general labor team performed a variety of functions, including cleaning. On some crews, such as laundry and dry cleaning, white and black students had the same duties. However, they performed them on different days of the week to maintain racial segregation. But some jobs seemed to fall to one racial group or the other. For example, black students did the bulk of the farming, logging, sawmill operations, and other dangerous and heavy fieldwork.

Each of Dozier's farm crews had about twenty black inmates and an adult black supervisor. Each morning the boys walked to the barn. From there, they rode into the fields in wagons pulled by tractors. Agricultural tasks ranged from clearing land and preparing soil, to planting, weeding, fertilizing, and harvesting crops. Dozier's main crops included corn, sugarcane, peas, and beans. Older boys trained the younger children and helped them with harder tasks. To pick corn, for example, taller boys pulled the cornstalks low so younger boys could pull off the corncobs. Older boys cut down sugarcane with sharp hoe blades, and younger ones gathered the cut stalks to remove their sharp leaves. After a day's work under the hot Florida sun, a boy's hands were raw, with cuts and blisters from the sharp leaves of the crops and from handling heavy equipment.

Black inmates on Dozier farm crews were required to do heavy agricultural labor and were often made to perform dangerous tasks unsuited to their age.

On other days, farming crews headed to nearby swamps, where boys helped convert the marshy areas to farmland. Crews usually did this work during colder months before and after the growing seasons. Temperatures during the cold season were not much above freezing, so standing in swamp water left boys numb and nearly frostbitten. In the morning, a crew might build a fire to help the boys warm up, but heating nearly frostbitten hands too quickly could do more harm than good. The swamp waters were also home to venomous snakes such as copperheads and cottonmouths. If a boy was bitten, the crew chief would cut the boy's wound open and try to squeeze the snake's poison out of the wound.

To clear trees from the marsh for timber, supervisors taught the boys to use heavy equipment such as chain saws. If the trees fell into the water, boys swam into water over their heads to tie ropes around the trunks to pull them out of the swamp. This was a dangerous task. Boys sometimes got caught between the felled logs, and the pressure of the heavy wood could break an arm or leg. At least one former student

Child Labor Laws

In 1904 the National Child Labor Committee was created. It exposed the injustice, cruelty, and harm of child labor. At this time in American history, about two million children worked long hours at difficult and dangerous jobs for very little pay. Finally, in 1924 the US Congress drafted a constitutional amendment to protect workers under the age of eighteen. However, few states ratified (approved) the amendment. In 1938 Congress instead passed the Fair Labor Standards Act, which governs employees under the age of eighteen to this day. The law outlines the acceptable and legal roles and working hours for minors. Work hours must not interfere with a child's education, for example. It is also illegal to hire a child under the age of fourteen for wages. Exceptions include paper routes, child actors, and parents who pay their children to help with household tasks.

One gap in the law was (and still is) agricultural work. Because of this gap, Dozier School was able to work young men in its farming operations. Even in the 1950s and 1960s, many of the children at Dozier were treated like slaves and worked in completely unsafe conditions. Boys as young as thirteen were expected to drive tractors. Some who were even younger felled trees, sawed logs, and performed other dangerous tasks. If boys were hurt, staff at the school's hospital often patched them up and sent them right back to work. According to author and slavery expert Antoinette Harrell, "The [Dozier] boys' human and civil rights were violated by the State of Florida."

reported that Dozier medical staff would set the fractures and send the boys right back to work with their casts on.

EDUCATION AT DOZIER

In the late 1950s, Frank Zych was the school principal. He had been a student at Dozier in the 1930s and was a varsity football star there. When he was released, he stayed in Marianna and played for the local high school team. Zych's football career ended when he lost his leg in a car accident late in his junior year. After earning his diploma from Marianna High School, Zych went to the University of Florida, earned his college degree, and returned to Dozier to teach and coach. Zych was one of the school's success stories, and he believed in the school's mission.

At Dozier, each boy's academic plan was based on initial testing rather than his age. So a sixth-grade class might have boys ranging in age from twelve to seventeen years. If a boy did exceptionally well in his class or if he did poorly, a teacher could request a change of grade or ask for the boy to be retested. Dozier used the same state-approved textbooks as public schools. And the boys studied with manuals produced by students in Dozier's own printshop. Boys worked at their own pace to complete pages in the school manuals.

Instruction focused on basic school subjects typical of various grades. First, second, and third graders had their classes together in one room. Fourth through eighth grades were each in their own classroom. Some tenth graders were in with the ninth-grade students, while other tenth graders were in with the combined eleventh- and twelfth-grade students. Teachers decided when students were ready to be promoted to the next grade level. Some students took and passed the General Education Development (GED) test at the school's guidance center, earning the equivalent of a high-school diploma.

Former student Arthur Huntley arrived at Dozier School in 1959, when he was twelve years old. He does not remember if he took a test to determine his grade, but he does recall he could not yet read or write. Huntley had an older brother, Willie Huntley, who had been at Dozier before him. He also had a younger brother named Richard Huntly (who spells his last name differently), who was at school with him. Arthur is not sure but believes he most likely started out in the fourth grade, and Richard, who was eleven, was put in the third grade.

The two younger brothers had been sent to Dozier School after their father died. Living in deep poverty, the family could not afford decent clothes, so the boys skipped school out of embarrassment. Their mother couldn't persuade them to stay in school—and out of trouble. So the local truant officer (an official who works with children who skip school) talked their mother into sending her boys to Dozier. The officer convinced Mrs. Huntley that her sons would be educated at Dozier and become good citizens. The officer also reassured her that her two boys would be together and be housed, fed, and clothed and that they would write home often. But once at the school, Arthur rarely saw Richard. Boys at Dozier were assigned to cottages according to age. And the brothers alternated school days and workdays, never on the same schedule. Though Richard was at the school for nearly two and a half years, he never made it from third to fourth grade.

SEPARATE AND NOT EQUAL

Boys were exhausted from days of hard work in the farm fields. Many lived in fear and were homesick for their families. Boys often did not get enough sleep and would fall asleep in school. If a boy misbehaved, the teacher might beat his knuckles with a wooden ruler. Or the teacher might grind his own knuckles into a boy's forehead. Any boy who had difficulty learning for whatever reason fell further and further behind.

Johnny Lee Gaddy was admitted to Dozier in 1957, also for skipping school. He spent five years there, from the age of eleven to sixteen. He says about the failings of his education at Dozier, "You know, I can't . . . I can't really read anything, I can see a word and kind of understand it, and I never could write anything down, you know, spell it out." Gaddy remembers the negative attitude of teachers at the school. He says that one schoolmaster told him and other black students that when they left Dozier and returned home, they would surely mess up again. The teacher said that since the boys were only being prepared for a future in prison, they didn't need to learn much of anything.

Racism and prejudice impacted Gaddy and the other nonwhite boys at Dozier. According to some sources, white boys received a much better education. They also generally started out at higher grade levels

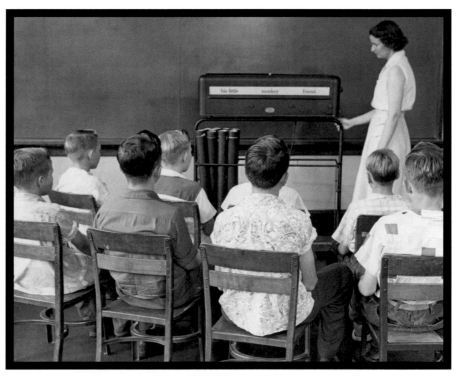

A reading teacher works with her class at Dozier. The school promised to provide a good education to all its students. Yet investigations and testimony from survivors show that white children received better training than black students. Some survivors feel the school broke its educational promise.

Sunup to Sundown

than the black children. Some white boys received far more training toward future careers. Images of the school from the 1950s show white students learning about mechanics and the new field of electronics, including radio and television. In the school's vocational programs, which were mostly for white students, tests and projects were used to document progress. The same was not always true of other programs.

Students, regardless of race, were sometimes taught the same skills—but never in a mixed-race setting. For example, Dozier had industrial arts courses in which students learned to use a variety of hand tools, power saws, arc welders, and spray painters. They learned to make ceramics and enamels. The school also had an art shop for students with talents in painting or drawing. Art projects included scenery for plays and other shows. Students also made lamps, picture frames, and signage for the campus. Other projects were gifts for family members or handicrafts the boys could keep for themselves.

Those with less talent and many black students ended up being trained in not much more than dry-cleaning or food service tasks. Some white boys felt they, too, were denied the education Dozier promised to deliver. For example, former student Roger Dean Kiser wrote, "I knew nothing about the outside world [when I left Dozier] and I knew nothing about life, at least about life outside an institution. . . . I didn't have any skills, except for how to press uniforms. I didn't even know where money came from or how you get it. . . . No one ever took the time to teach us anything about the real world. They just fed us, clothed us, housed us, and educated us in the basic subjects."

ESCAPEES

Life at Dozier was demanding and often brutal. Some students tried to escape. Yet many did not. They recall that the fear of what would happen to them if they ran away or if they spoke up about mistreatment kept them silent and prevented them from fleeing. The dreadful punishments for attempted escape were notorious. Stories of the horrible penalties for escape passed among the students, striking terror in all who heard them.

If a cottage had no runaways in a given period of time, all residents in the group earned a reward such as a trip to the nearby ocean beach. But if a boy tried to escape, the whole cottage had to wait a year for such privileges. If school officials caught a runaway, they might first return him to the cottage, knowing that his dormitory mates would likely take revenge for the punishment he had brought down on the entire group. They might force the boy to walk down a line of fellow residents who would beat him with their belts. Some were so angry they would hit the runaway in the head, rather than on his backside.

The escapee would then face further punishment by school staff at a legendary building known as the "white house." There the most severe and horrific discipline took place. In some cases, an escapee's work crew or cottage mates never saw the runaway again. They would often be told he had been discharged from the school and taken home. But the boys all knew that no one was ever sent home after an escape attempt. That just made no sense at all, not even to a child.

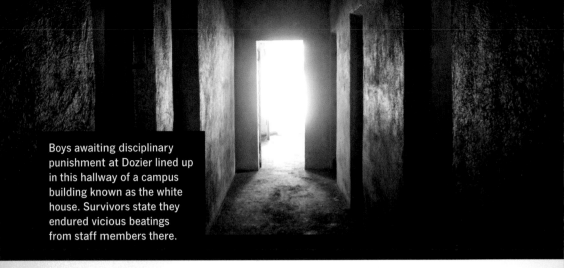

Boys awaiting disciplinary punishment at Dozier lined up in this hallway of a campus building known as the white house. Survivors state they endured vicious beatings from staff members there.

Chapter 3
THE WHITE HOUSE

Dozier boys described it as a pair of leather straps, each several inches wide. The straps were fastened along their length to a thin sheet of flexible metal of the same width. A piece of wood at one end of the straps served as the handle. Some boys later described holes in the leather that sucked up skin and blood as the straps hit a boy's skin. Survivors say they were hit so hard that the force of the blow pushed their bodies nearly 1 foot (0.3 m) into the cot mattress on which they were lying. Others described how deeply the metal insert could cut into flesh, if the belt turned sideways during a beating.

Survivors remember the foul smell of old saliva, sweat, vomit, and urine on the cot mattress and pillow. Both bore bloodstains and bits of tissue from boys who had bitten their lips and tongues to endure the pain and keep from screaming. Some inmates would bite down on the filthy pillow just to keep from crying out. The staff told boys not to scream. Some survivors think it was easier for staff to abuse the boys if they didn't cry out to show the depth of their pain. They believe their cries might have reached whatever remaining humanity the staff had. Some former Dozier inmates said they learned to scream only on the inside.

If a boy cried out or tried to get up, or if he let go of the cot's rail, the staff member would start counting the number of blows again, from the beginning. Some boys lost count of how many times they were struck. Others will never forget that number. After a beating, most boys returned to their cottages limping, with bruised and bloody buttocks. Some had to go to the hospital, where medical staff removed bits of underwear from the wounds with tweezers. The tougher victims might brag about how many hits they took. Others could hardly speak of it. It is alleged that some boys who made a trip to the white house were never seen again. Cottage fathers would say the boy went home, when the other kids knew he didn't have a home to go to. In addition, boys couldn't be released until they had at least achieved the rank of pioneer level, and some of the boys who disappeared were not yet at that ranking.

During the 1950s, Dozier's psychologist, Dr. Eugene Byrd, had received enough complaints from students that he asked to witness a "spanking" session by staff at the school. Years later, in 1958, Byrd testified before the US Senate Judiciary Subcommittee during its study of juvenile delinquency. Byrd described the "spanking" he witnessed at Dozier. "The blows are very severe. They are dealt with a great deal of force with a full arm swing over [the] head and down, with a strap, a leather strap approximately a half inch [1.3 cm] thick and about 10 inches [25 cm] long with a wooden formed handle." Byrd concluded, "In my personal opinion, it is brutality."

"I Didn't Have to Kill You"

"So he hit me the first time and I jumped up, and he slapped me upside my ear with the belt and said, 'N*****, you get back down there, I'm going to kill you.' I'm scared to death, I ain't never been hit like that in my life, so I got back down on the bed and he began to hit me, and I flinch . . . I can feel . . . my flesh coming off my body through my pants every time he hit me, he had holes in this belt . . . and when he hit me, he sucked the skin from my body and I couldn't even get up off the bed, he had to come and help me get off the bed, and I was so bloody, my behind was full of blood, and he kept telling me that 'You did good . . . you did good. . . . I didn't have to kill you.'"

—Johnny Lee Gaddy

THE TORTURE CHAMBER

On Dozier's south side, where the white boys lived, was the white house. A cinder block building erected in 1929 and painted white, it originally had ten small windows. Workers later blocked off nine of the windows on the inside and outside, leaving only a small grated area near the top through which light could pass. Former Dozier students of the 1950s through the 1970s refer to the white house as a torture chamber. It was where boys were brutally punished with an implement like the strap Byrd described in his testimony.

The white house had a front door and another on its left side. The front door opened into a main room that had one small window. The room also had four big windows, one on either side of the door, and one on each side of the building. A hallway ran straight down the center of the building. Smaller rooms opened off the hallway. A large, industrial fan in the hallway ceiling made a great deal of noise. Staff turned it on during beatings to cover the screams of the victims, according to survivors. But those who had once waited in that hallway as boys report that the fan did not hide the sounds of the abuse.

FACEDOWN AND HOLD THE RAIL

Staff members took boys to the white house for discipline. When serious or even minor incidents of misbehavior occurred, staff instructed the offending boys to line up in the center of the long hallway. Some said being first in line—closest to the "torture chamber" near the end of the hallway—was better. This was because those at the back of the line heard the lashes and cries of all the boys who went before them. The anxiety increased the brutality of the punishment. Other survivors said it was better to be last in line since by the time the first few boys were beaten, the abusers were exhausted and couldn't swing as hard. Sometimes the men who beat the boys would take turns. Survivors allege the staff joked or made bets among themselves to see who could make a child bleed with the first stroke.

The similarity among accounts of experiencing, witnessing, or being forced to participate in brutal beatings in the white house help verify the stories of survivors.

Corporal Punishment

Corporal punishment is a form of discipline in which one person causes bodily trauma and pain to another person. In the United States and many other parts of the world, corporal punishment was common during the centuries of slavery. It was also common in schools and in some families. In many US schools, a teacher used a flexible wooden rod called a switch, both to point at things on the blackboard and to spank students. The switch was usually made of birch, cane (such as sugarcane), hazel, hickory, or willow. To spank a student, the teacher would place the child on his or her lap to receive blows on the backside. In other cases, the teacher would strike the child's palms. Paddles with a handle eventually replaced switches for school "spankings" in the principal's office. There, a student would lean over a desk or chair to receive the punishment.

In 1867 New Jersey became the first state to outlaw corporal punishment in schools. It was more than one hundred years before a second state—Massachusetts—banned physical discipline in schools in 1971. By 2018 thirty-one states had abolished corporal punishment in public schools. Of the nineteen that still allow it, a majority are southern states.

Public school systems can choose to outlaw physical discipline even if their state still permits it. Only New Jersey and Iowa also prohibit corporal punishment in private schools. Research collected by the US Department of Education indicated that in the 2013–2014 school year (the most recent for which data are available), 110,000 US students received corporal punishment in K–12 schools. Studies indicate that males are more than three times more likely than females to be physically disciplined. Black students of both sexes and students with disabilities are more often subject to corporal punishment than other students. As of 2016, corporal punishment is outlawed in K–12 schools in all European countries, as well as in many parts of South America and Asia.

In this image from 2009, Dozier survivor Dick Colon holds a replica of one of the several types of instruments said to have been used over the school's history to beat inmates.

As a boy entered the room for his punishment, the man giving the beating told him to untuck his shirt, unbutton his trousers, and lie face down on the cot. Then he told the boy to reach over his head and hold onto the rail at the top of the cot. Most importantly, the boy was not to let go during the beating. If he did, or if he looked back at his abuser or to see what he was being hit with, he earned additional blows.

Staff forced some boys to assist in and witness the brutal punishments. One survivor, Arthur Huntley, reported that staff sometimes made him hold down the lower legs of the smaller boys who couldn't stay still during a beating. He didn't like doing it, but he told himself that maybe it helped the younger ones avoid more blows. Huntley himself had been a victim of beatings and knew the pain. He also knew he would get another beating if he didn't follow orders and hold the boys down. Survivors remember that the staff didn't seem to care if a boy was healed from the last whipping before giving him another one. Some youngsters received beatings that ripped the scabs from their last trip to the white house right off their backsides.

In the days after a beating, a boy often carried a pillow to the cafeteria to cushion his brutalized buttocks. The pillow was also a

The White House

warning sign to other boys. All had heard stories about the beatings, and to see a boy with a pillow was a frightening reminder of the intense suffering at the white house. Almost worse, the pillow was a powerful symbol of humiliation and shame. It went along with questions from the other boys such as, "Did you hold the rail?" or "How many hits did you take?"

THE BLUE GOOSE

The white house was on the south side of the campus where the white students lived, so they saw it every day as they walked to the dining hall. When a white boy was "taken down," as a trip to the white house was called, staff typically marched him there. However, when black students were scheduled for a beating, and occasionally in the case of white students, staff usually drove them to the white house in a car they called the Blue Goose. In the late 1950s, Dozier and other public institutions were racially segregated by law. So at Dozier, black employees could only punish black boys, while white staff were allowed to "spank" either black or white students. In fact, the white house had two separate rooms for beatings—one for black children and one for white.

WHAT DID THE TOWN KNOW?

To some outsiders, everything at Dozier looked just fine. But the school was not isolated, so some people knew or suspected the harsh truth. For example, about 150 local people from Marianna had jobs at Dozier. Many of their relatives had worked there too. Dozier students with privileges went to the town's movie theater and skating rink, and the Marianna and Dozier varsity sports teams met on the playing fields.

Each year at the county fair, the school's farm exhibited its prized produce and livestock. Local farmers were invited to come to Dozier to learn about the school's agricultural program. Marianna school groups could even tour the facility to learn about reforming and training wayward youth. At Christmas every year, the local community was invited to drive through Dozier's elaborate holiday lights and campus decorations. The townspeople were also invited each Easter morning to worship at the campus's segregated religious services.

Elmore Bryant was Marianna's first African American mayor. He was born in 1934, grew up near the school, and was a teacher at Dozier for a short time in the early 1990s. Bryant tells a different story about the community around the school. He remembers that kids in his neighborhood lived in fear of being sent to Dozier. Parents and teachers would threaten boys, telling them that if they didn't behave, they would wind up at Dozier. Bryant knew neighborhood boys who had been sent to Dozier and returned with tales of dangerous, hard labor and severe beatings.

THE FEAR OF SPEAKING OUT

Some people wonder why Dozier boys didn't speak out about their abuse at the time or at least try to flee the school, especially since it was not fenced. Like many victims of abuse, their humiliation kept them silent prisoners. The people who were supposed to take care of these boys were hurting them, so they felt hopeless with nowhere to turn. They were also terrified that by speaking out or trying to escape, they would face even more punishment. Everyone at Dozier knew what happened to boys who got caught in an escape attempt.

Additionally, escaping Dozier was hard. Swampland and forested areas surrounded the school. If a boy took an escape route through the wooded areas, he ended up on roads that led directly to Marianna. He knew that when the Dozier sirens blared to announce a runaway, some town residents and local farmers would park their vehicles on those roads. They would turn off their vehicle headlights as they waited to capture the unsuspecting fugitive. Anyone who caught and turned in an escapee earned a reward—goods from the school's farms and maybe even fifty dollars. And Dozier officials warned residents of Marianna not to help or protect runaway boys. Some townspeople may have wanted to help but were afraid to do so.

If a boy chose to escape into the swamps rather than the forest, he was sure to face snakes, alligators, and other dangers. The school's guards didn't like to go into the swamp, so in some cases, authorities used "dog boys" to chase down runaways. These men from the local prison handled tracking dogs to hunt down boys who had escaped. Some captured children returned to the school covered in dog bites and were heard screaming as shower water sprayed down on their wounds. Survivors claim supervisors sometimes forced captured boys to get down on their hands and knees to kiss the tracking dog's rear end or its genitals—and the men would laugh while the boys performed this act.

RUNNER IN THE SWAMP

When Robert Straley was at Dozier, he worked as a hospital boy. Each day he did routine chores such as mopping floors. As time went on, he was given more responsibilities, including giving shots with a hypodermic needle and learning to stitch up a cut. One day, Straley came across a boy in one of the clinic beds. The boy was shaking all over and his face was pale, as though he were in shock. Blood-soaked towels applied to his skin covered much of his body.

The next day, as Straley was changing clothes in the hospital's linen closet, he overheard some men on the other side of the door. One man told the others that the "runner," as boys who escaped were called, would end up in the swamp and would not be coming back to Dozier. The boy had tried to escape one too many times, he said, and the school was done with it. The next day, the bloodied boy was gone. Straley knew that the boy had been too severely wounded to have been released from the hospital. But he also knew not to ask questions. He never saw the boy again. He always wondered if the men had taken the boy out to the swamp and left him there to die.

If a boy disappeared, Dozier officials would send parents a letter from the school's superintendent. The letter informed them that their son had run away and not been found. Some parents questioned this; others did not. Some boys had no family to worry about them or to wonder about their whereabouts. Dozier had control of these children. Saying the boys ran away from the school was a simple explanation for a disappearance that was difficult for a family to challenge. Without witnesses to Dozier's many secrets, the fates of the boys who ran away, or who simply disappeared from the school, may never be known.

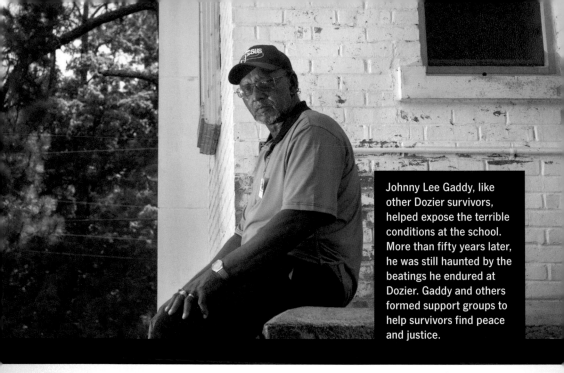

Johnny Lee Gaddy, like other Dozier survivors, helped expose the terrible conditions at the school. More than fifty years later, he was still haunted by the beatings he endured at Dozier. Gaddy and others formed support groups to help survivors find peace and justice.

Chapter 4

"WE WERE JUST KIDS"

By the early twenty-first century, individuals had begun to publicly acknowledge and describe the savagery they had experienced at Dozier School. When they began to share their stories, most of them were men between fifty-five and seventy years of age who had been at Dozier in the 1950s and 1960s. The similarities among their personal accounts helped to establish the truth of the stories.

Dozier survivors came forward for various reasons. Some wanted to face their abusers and seek justice for the harm they had suffered.

Many felt that coming forward, to acknowledge what had happened in their youth might aid in their healing. Many hoped that sharing their stories would help ensure that experiences such as theirs do not happen again. Some men witnessed others come forward, and it gave them the courage to tell their own stories. By binding themselves to other men who understood their pain, the "boys" of Dozier became men who found strength, safety, and comfort in their brotherhood.

Because these men were haunted by their memories of the school, many kept their horrific experiences secret for decades. The incidents of abuse cost some survivors their mental well-being, their ability to trust others, their emotional stability, their marriages, their livelihoods, or combinations of such losses. Life at Dozier was supposed to reform children and help them grow into competent adults. Instead, it stripped some of their psychological health, their sense of worth and dignity, their ability to bond with others, and the capacity to fully participate in society.

No matter how boys behaved at the school or what they may have done that caused them to be sentenced to Dozier, the students were all minors. They were children who had few adults to support or advocate for them. These youngsters knew little or nothing about their rights. Some had broken laws and been sent to Dozier. Others were simply mischievous. None deserved the injustices they suffered at the school.

Before coming to Dozier, many had already endured some of the worst hardships that children can experience—the loss of parents, child abuse or neglect that caused them to run away from home, or disabilities that led them to have serious problems in school. Some had aligned themselves with the wrong set of "friends." Others were simply in the wrong place at the wrong time. Many men share the pains that were common to Dozier survivors before, during, and after their time at the school. Each has his own heartbreaking story. In banding together, some of these men found the strength to acknowledge these wrongs and tell others what happened to them as children.

JOHNNY LEE GADDY

Johnny Lee Gaddy grew up in Dade City, Florida. He had a speech impediment as a child and was often bullied. When the bullying got to be too much, he would skip school. So in 1957, when he was eleven years old, he was picked up for truancy (being absent from school without an authorized reason) and put in jail. Authorities told Gaddy he would go before a judge who would determine a suitable punishment. But instead, he was sent straight to Dozier. Gaddy was told he would be at Dozier for six months. He says that a police officer told him, "That's a good school, they'll teach you a lot up there." But instead of six months, Gaddy was at Dozier for five years of hard labor. In addition, the school at Marianna was five hours from his home, and no one from his family came to visit him there. Gaddy's father had already died. His mother could not read or write and had thirteen other children to raise.

As a boy, Gaddy liked to hunt and was not afraid of snakes and alligators. He thinks Dozier staff put him in the swamp to clear land for farming because of this. Gaddy found it hard to believe that the school would even think of putting crops in the swamp. Working against the high water levels and clearing the marshy land to grow crops didn't make sense to him. All the same, Gaddy and the other

> **"What I want is for the truth to come out. We know what we saw. I know what I saw. It can't be denied. I wish it hadn't happened, but it did happen to me while I was at that school as a child. I still wonder at 67 years old, why me? I can't understand it. . . . We were under a lot of threats when we went to Marianna as young boys. . . . I learned . . . how to shut my mouth—because I wanted to survive. I wanted to go home."**
>
> *—Johnny Lee Gaddy*

black boys at Dozier cleared the trees, cut up the lumber, helped haul it away, and planted crop seeds. They were soon picking corn, peas, beans, and other produce. By the time Gaddy was thirteen, the supervisors had him driving a tractor in the swamp fields. He himself supervised crews of younger boys in the fields.

As he got older, Gaddy looked out for the younger kids at Dozier. He tried to comfort them when they wanted their mama or daddy and when they asked why they were being treated worse than animals. In the fields, Gaddy worked hard to keep his whole crew from going to the white house. He cautioned the little boys, "You got to work, man, and you got to keep your mouth closed, because if you don't they are going to kill you."

One day Gaddy was out in the swamp to clear land with other boys from the Robinson cottage. Clearing land meant wading into deep swamp water to cut down trees. The boys put the trees on a trailer so they could be taken to the campus sawmill. The crew chief assigned Gaddy and a much smaller, younger boy to handle either end of a long, two-man saw. The smaller boy was too short to be standing in the deep water, and he wasn't strong enough to handle one end of the saw. So Gaddy had to do the work of pushing the saw and then pulling it back. The younger boy begged Gaddy not to tell the crew chief. Knowing the risks to the younger child if the chief were to see he was not working the saw, Gaddy kept quiet. It felt good looking out for others, and it was one of only a few ways of making any boy at Dozier feel worthwhile.

Gaddy says that when he finally got home, he told his brothers to do anything in their power to avoid going to Dozier. Gaddy's mother did not understand his strong feelings about Dozier. She said that the school's administrators had always reported that he was doing just fine. One letter home did mention that Gaddy had received a "spanking." Gaddy says, "My mother had no idea that 'spanking' meant my body was being practically torn in half." He tried to tell her about the severity of the abuse, but she had trouble believing it. She insisted she received nothing but good reports from the school. When he asked why she had never visited, she said the Dozier staff told her that if she came to visit, she might damage her son's progress in the school's rigorous rehabilitation program.

Survivors such as Gaddy often faced disbelief when they shared their memories of what had happened to them at Dozier. Families often chose not to believe the horrors. Or, like Gaddy's mother, they had received a different version of events from the school itself. In fact, Gaddy's daughter was eventually able to obtain her father's Dozier records from the State of Florida. They indicate that Johnny Lee Gaddy was only at the school for nine months (January through September 1959). Yet he was actually there for five long years. The records also say that Gaddy was in the school's glee club. However, Gaddy says he had no idea what a glee club was while at the school. As for the educational opportunities he was promised at the school, Gaddy says he learned a lot about hard work. He can drive a tractor and mow grass well. But during his five years at the Dozier School, he was never given the opportunity to learn to read.

ROBERT W. STRALEY

Robert Straley was an only child. He grew up in a rural area outside of Tampa, Florida. From an early age, the boy felt his mother's resentment toward him, especially when she would show him the scar on her belly from his caesarean birth (a surgical procedure in which a mother's womb is cut open to remove the baby). She told Straley he had ruined her figure and forever ended her possibility of an acting career. His mother also displayed sudden outbreaks of hostility and other irrational behaviors that left him wondering what he had done to upset her and why she treated him so badly.

Straley's father was a truck driver who was gone much of the time. The boy was sure his father traveled to get away from his wife's

"You could hear grunts, and then groans, and then that turned into screams, and just 'Oh God, help me, mama,' you know, and just noises I had never heard before; people in real pain. And, I guess you would have had to been a person that was in war, or an ambulance attendant or something like that, to really hear people screaming like that. . . . And they just led me in there. It was like being in a dream that you couldn't stop for some reason."

—Robert Straley

domination and rage. One night, when Straley and his mother were home alone, she woke her son, with a pistol in hand, saying someone was trying to break in. He watched as she opened the front door, shot a man on the porch, closed the door, and returned to bed. The next day, police found the man dead, just a short distance from the Straley home.

Straley began to run away from home to escape his mother's unpredictability and verbal abuse. The police would find him and return him to his home with a warning. When Straley was thirteen, his mother refused to take him back after the police brought him home from another runaway attempt. So Straley was sent to the Dozier School in March 1963 for a sentence of one year. He weighed only 105 pounds (48 kg), had never once been in a fight, and had only occasionally been away from home. On the bus to Marianna, Straley and other boys were chained by their ankles and wrists. The older boys intimidated him, even though he saw fear in their eyes too.

At the Dozier administrative office, staff removed the chains from Straley's ankles and wrists. A tall man named Mr. Hatton registered him and gave him a uniform. A staff member took Straley to Lincoln cottage on the white campus. He was impressed by the tidiness of the cottage, with its thirty cots in three, neat rows. The cottage had a Ping-Pong

Robert Straley remembers the abuse he suffered when he was an inmate at Dozier. Straley was one of the first of the Dozier survivors to go public with his memories of what had happened to him at the institution.

table, a television, and a reading room, and the bright white paint gleamed. Straley was shown to his bunk and was then led to the cafeteria for dinner. He had no idea that within hours his first impression of Dozier's neat and tidy appearance would be completely shattered.

Before dinner, as he was trying to make friends, Straley spoke briefly with three boys seated on a bench outside Lincoln cottage. To his surprise, they were discussing plans to run away from the school. Straley quickly walked away and didn't think much about it after that. Not while eating beans and potatoes at dinner, not when getting into his bunk for his first night's sleep at the reform school. It wasn't until a man stuck a flashlight in his face and told him to get out of bed that Straley realized he was in trouble. The three boys from the bench that day were being rousted from their bunks too.

The man marched Straley and the other three Dozier inmates outside and toward a car. The boys were clothed in nothing but their underwear. Hatton, the tall man who had registered Straley earlier that day, was there. So was a short, stocky, one-armed man named Mr. Tidwell. As the men pushed Straley into the car, he told them that he was not planning to run away with the others. The one-armed man jerked him out of the vehicle and barked into his face that he was not to speak unless he was spoken to first. Then he shoved Straley into the back seat again. Within minutes the car stopped in front of the white house, and Straley and the other three boys were taken in. Straley was forced to watch as the men dragged the three other boys into another room, one at a time. The men switched on a large industrial ceiling fan, but Straley still heard the muffled screams of the boys as they were beaten. And he saw their battered bodies as they emerged, blood dripping from their tattered underwear and down their legs, their faces streaked with tears.

When it was Straley's turn, the men pulled him into the small room, where he saw blood on the mattress and walls. They forced him onto the mattress, and Hatton told Straley to turn his face to the wall and bite down on the filthy pillow. Tidwell began to beat Straley. Sweating and with eyeglasses half-cocked, Tidwell's body twisted with each wail of the belt. With each whack, Straley could hear the soles of Tidwell's shoes scraping against the floor. Straley counted thirty lashes before he lost consciousness. When he regained consciousness, in excruciating pain, he found himself in the shower at Lincoln cottage. This was Robert Straley's first night at Dozier.

RICHARD HUNTLY

Richard Huntly had a difficult and complex childhood. His parents were separated, and he did not know his mother until after his father died in 1954, when Richard was eight. Huntly's oldest brother, Willie, was already in Dozier School at that time. The reform school released Willie to attend his father's funeral. After that, Willie was put up for adoption, so Richard never really knew his older brother. After their father's death, Richard and his other siblings were taken to their mother's home and left on her porch with their few belongings.

The children sat on the porch for some time, waiting for their mother to come home from work. She took them in to live with the

Richard Huntly, one of the founders of the support group Black Boys at Dozier Reform School, was one of three brothers in the same family who ended up at Dozier. Of his experience there, he says it scarred him emotionally for life.

additional children she had from another relationship. Richard's mother worked, but her earnings were not enough to support the large household. So the family soon found themselves turning to social services agencies for help. Huntly remembers hard times when the only food they had to eat was whatever the boys could scrounge out of the local garbage dump. Without adequate clothing, the boys were teased at school. Embarrassed by their poverty, the brothers stopped attending school. From time to time, the police were involved in their truancy. Eventually a truant officer picked them up and told their mother her best option was to send them to Dozier. The officer promised her that her sons would be educated, fed, and housed.

So in May 1957, eleven-year-old Richard Huntly and his brother Arthur were sent to Dozier. Huntly recalls a total of four beatings during his time at Dozier between 1957 and 1959. In his words, "I begged, cried, moaned, and groaned. There are no words to describe that sudden severe pain administered to your body. I had an out-of-body experience. I think I honestly left my body and the pain there on that cot."

Nearly as horrific as the beatings was the intense and dangerous physical work Huntly's young body was forced to endure day after day. He was part of a Dozier sugarcane crew, working from "can to can't." The boys used this phrase to refer to the long hours they worked in the fields, from the time they could see at daylight until the time they could no longer see as the sun went down. Cutting sugarcane meant working with sharp hoes and other dangerous tools. Harvesttime was during the cold winter months. Huntly was so cold one day that he could hardly feel his extremities. When his freshly sharpened hoe hit the top of his right foot, he barely felt any pain. But as the blood streamed from his boot, he knew it was bad. After removing his footwear, he saw that most of his toe was gone. Huntly says he sat on the cold ground and cried—not because of the pain but because of his helplessness. At Dozier he had no one to care for him.

After the accident, the school staff transferred Huntly to Dozier's meat processing plant and slaughterhouse, where he again worked with sharp, dangerous implements. His job was to participate in killing livestock (cattle and pigs), including animals that were many times his own body weight. Huntly helped corral the animals into a holding chute. He used an electric prod to shock the more stubborn animals

"On one side (the black side) we did the planting, we did the killing, we prepared everything for the white side. . . . We just worked. . . . The trades we learned were how to drive a tractor, how to plant in the fields, how to cut cane. My toe got cut off when I was eleven years old trying to cut cane for making syrup and sugar. I understand that on the other side, they never saw any of this kind of work. But on the black side, we had no choice but to play the role of a slave, a child slave."

−Richard Huntly

"We Were Just Kids"

into moving into the chute, while trying to keep out of their way. He was often knocked down into a mixture of mud, blood, urine, and feces on the slaughterhouse floor. Fifty years later, Huntly said he could still smell the blood of that slaughterhouse.

Once an animal was in the holding pen, an adult worker would shoot the animal between its eyes with a rifle. If the animal suddenly moved and the gun missed, the man with the rifle would continue to fire bullets until the animal was down. Then another adult worker would come in and cut the animal open with a knife and hang it up to allow its blood to drain out. Huntly realized—especially when he was in the pen with cattle—that if an animal turned on him before the worker killed it, there would be no time for others to jump in to save him. Not that Huntly believed anyone would try to help. He figured if he did die in the slaughterhouse, the school would not admit it had put a young boy—even a black boy like him—in such danger. He figured he would likely wind up as just another kid who disappeared from Dozier.

ROGER DEAN KISER

When Roger Dean Kiser was just four years old, his mother abandoned him and his younger half sister and their two-week-old brother. When the police found the children four days after their mother's disappearance, the baby was dead in Kiser's arms. The authorities contacted the father of Kiser's half sister. He took the two children to live with his parents.

The couple were cruel to Kiser. One day when he crossed the street to play in the nearby schoolyard, teachers saw Kiser's "grandmother" come over, swinging a leather strap and screaming at the boy to get home. Kiser was so scared that he soiled his pants. His grandmother dragged him back to the house by his ear. His "grandfather" saw the mess in Kiser's pants, rubbed it in his face, and sent the child to the yard to be hosed down. Meanwhile, the teachers called authorities, who found Kiser naked in the backyard.

Survivor Roger Dean Kiser was among the men who founded the White House Boys support group. He and others spoke of their experiences at Dozier at a 2008 ceremony to recognize the suffering of survivors. Kiser says the humiliation and psychological abuse he endured at the school were more damaging to him than the physical abuse.

Because of the abuse, and without relatives to care for him, Kiser became a ward of the State of Florida. He spent the next seven years in two different orphanages, where he was abused mentally, physically, and sexually. He frequently ran away from these horrors, living on the streets until authorities found him and sent him back. Kiser eventually ended up in juvenile court as a chronic runaway. The judge sentenced Kiser to Dozier School in 1959 for being "unable to follow instructions" and for being "incorrigible." Kiser later commented, "My true crime, my real 'crime,' was not having parents to care for me."

Kiser arrived at Dozier in the summer of 1959, when he was twelve years old. He spent two different terms at Dozier and says the years all blended in his memory as one long nightmare. While at the school, Kiser was sent to psychological counseling with a man called Dr. Currie. Currie was neither a medical doctor nor a licensed psychologist, and boys warned Kiser that Currie was strange. From the first meeting, Currie regularly questioned Kiser about how often he (or other boys) masturbated. He once demanded that Kiser pull down his pants to demonstrate exactly how he played with himself, claiming that masturbation was the source of Kiser's problems. The boy took down his pants, feeling ashamed, alone, and afraid for his life. Currie shouted at Kiser, calling him a freak and a pervert and ordering him to pull up his pants and get out of his office. The mind games and unpredictability were part of Currie's particular brand of torture.

Other staff at Dozier had different techniques of humiliation. For example, one day Hatton, the south-campus director, grabbed Kiser by the arm as they walked past each other and asked why the boy wasn't smiling. When Kiser replied that he was sad and didn't want to smile, Hatton slapped the boy across the face with full force. He screamed at him to get down on the ground and asked if Kiser would prefer a trip to the white house to a simple smile. Kiser apologized for not smiling at Hatton, and the encounter ended. A few days later, Kiser again saw Hatton and gave the man a big, toothy grin. Hatton yelled at the boy to wipe the smile off his face. He ordered him to head to the main office and wait to be taken down to the white house for punishment. Kiser sat in the office for what seemed like an eternity. When Hatton didn't show up, staff sent Kiser back to his cottage. All night and for several days after that, he waited for the beating, but it never came. While at Dozier, Kiser did experience two trips to the white house, but on this occasion, the torment was the waiting game.

PSYCHOLOGICAL ABUSE

When scheduled, beatings were usually set for Saturdays. During church services on Sundays, which were mandatory, the boys who had been battered the day before could hardly sit on the wooden pews. Kiser heard the preacher talk of brotherhood, love, and kindness while his abusers stood in the corners, eyeing the boys for any sign of misbehavior. When the preacher asked, as a regular part of the service, if anyone wanted to come to the front of the chapel and give his soul to God, Kiser felt he no longer had a soul. The orphanages and Dozier had taken it from him. In thinking about his life at Dozier, Kiser says he believes the psychological abuse he endured had a far more profound effect on him than the beatings at the white house did.

Part of the psychological harm that Kiser and other boys experienced

"It is bad enough to be a scared, lonely child. But even worse than that is becoming an adult with that same scared, lonely child still living inside. It is the feeling that inspired me to try to make a difference in the lives of children today by sharing my awful experiences, but also by sharing my triumphs despite those experiences. . . . Fortunately, there were a few people in my early life who touched my heart just enough so that I could eventually release the haunting memories of my childhood."

—Roger Dean Kiser

at Dozier came from witnessing the excruciating suffering of others. When Kiser worked at the school's hospital, he had to undress an injured boy and put his bloody, near-lifeless body into a bathtub to clean him. From the injuries, it appeared the boy had been mauled by dogs. Kiser told the nurse he didn't think he could bear to watch the boy die. She suggested simply that he leave the hospital crew if he couldn't perform his duties. So he transferred to the laundry and dry-cleaning facility. But he still saw tragedy on the job.

One afternoon, Kiser heard yelling and saw some boys being sent away from the laundry area. Then he saw staff carrying a bundle that looked like a body under a sheet to a waiting car and throwing the bundle into the vehicle. Kiser later heard that a black boy had cussed at the laundry supervisor, who ordered the other boys to put the young man in the dryer and tumble him. Other Dozier survivors corroborate this incident. In fact, one of them, Dick Colon, says he saw the boy's body flopping around in the dryer. Kiser believes that what he saw thrown in the car that day was the boy's body. If so, the psychological abuse perpetrated on boys at Dozier may have included supervisors forcing students to harm one another.

"We Were Just Kids"

SEXUAL ABUSE

Johnny Lee Gaddy is one of numerous men who have come forward to reveal that boys at Dozier were molested and raped. He remembers that for a time, a man would come to the Robinson cottage on the black side of campus several evenings a month. This man would tell the cottage father that he was taking one of the boys on an outing to the library, the gym, or somewhere else. Gaddy says this was a lie. The boys were taken from the cottage and molested.

Gaddy believes the Robinson cottage father knew what was going on and didn't try to stop it. Gaddy figured this out when a younger boy who had not been at Dozier long came back crying from one of the outings. The cottage father told the boy to take a shower. As the young man walked toward the bathroom, the other boys could see that he was bleeding from his rear end, right through his clothing. From this, Gaddy assumed the child had been raped. Gaddy says that younger boys were often chosen for these "outings." And when they returned, the others heard them crying in their bunks at night.

During his first year at Dozier, when Gaddy was eleven years old, the rapist chose him one night. He told Gaddy it was his turn to clean the office. When they got to the office, the man ordered Gaddy to take off his clothes, and he raped him. When the sexual assault was over, the rapist threatened Gaddy, telling the boy that if he told anyone, he would kill him. Gaddy says of his abuser, "He was really nasty. He could hurt you. He could hurt you really bad. He did some pretty bad things to the boys, he was crazy and we knew he was that way. . . . All the directors around knew, and they just covered up for him."

Gaddy finally got up the courage to tell his cottage father what was going on during the outings. The man accused him of lying, warning him of a beating if the school director learned of these lies. Gaddy realized at that moment he had nobody to trust, no one he could talk to about the terrible things that were happening to him—not even the man entrusted with his care and safety in the cottage they shared as their home.

Gaddy kept his silence until he was released from Dozier nearly five years later. He remembers that when he finally left the school, he tried to tell his mother of the beatings and rapes. "No one believed me, not even my mother. . . . We were boys and they would tell people that we were bad boys, so no one would believe us or listen to us. For a man to be raped and talk about it, it's very embarrassing. We were kids, and we were scared to death." So, like many victims of sexual abuse, Gaddy kept his experience to himself in secrecy, silence, and shame. His childhood days at Dozier continue to haunt him: "I'm still crying. . . . Fifty years later, I'm still crying. . . . I see something sad, I cry. I cried so many nights and days . . . for myself and the others."

THE RAPE ROOM

Gaddy was assaulted in the school's office. Dozier survivor Freddie Williams recalls being whipped on a cot in the white house by one man and then raped on the very same cot by another. That man sexually assaulted Williams over and over in the following months, giving him snacks and treats in trade for sex acts. Other survivors tell of a place at Dozier that boys called the "rape room." Some remember it as the crawl space beneath the dining hall, while others say they were taken to a cellar room beneath the school. Some survivors describe it as a room under the gymnasium. All agree it was a dark and dingy place with a mattress on the floor.

One night Tidwell and another Dozier staff member snatched Robert Straley and took him to the rape room. After years of trying to block out the memory, Straley was able to recall being facedown on the floor with a man on top of him. He could smell the man's rotten breath and hear him grunting as he raped him. Straley felt as if the bones in his chest might break from the weight of the grown man's body.

DR. SOUZA'S SOUP

During part of their time at Dozier, both Robert Straley and Roger Kiser worked at the school's hospital. They witnessed the medical staff treating boys who had been beaten. In not reporting the beatings to legal authorities, the school's medical personnel were complicit (involved) in the wrongdoing. They were also not fulfilling their ethical responsibilities to the boys. Former student Andrew Puel recalls the medical evaluation on his first day at Dozier. He and other boys were standing in a line, naked and fearful, waiting to be examined and vaccinated. One boy cried out in fear of the vaccination needle. Puel witnessed a doctor slap the boy's face, over and over, for being afraid.

Another form of medical malpractice at Dozier was later confirmed through testimony from both former students and staff members, including Tidwell. It involved Dr. Louis Souza (sometimes spelled Sousa), who was the staff psychiatrist at Dozier from the mid-1950s until the mid-1960s. Souza believed that behavioral disorders were related to an insufficient supply of oxygen in the blood. He hypothesized that feeding the children more protein might stimulate increased production of red blood cells, which carry oxygen in the blood. He also thought that the best years for treatment were when a person was between the ages of eleven and twenty-one. Souza looked to Dozier—an institution full of juvenile offenders—as a remarkable opportunity for experimentation. There he could work on behavioral disorders with a population of youths whose diet and other activities he could track and control.

So, Souza designed and administered his own high-protein liquid concoction made from red bone marrow— known as Dr. Souza's soup—to boys in his care. Then he drew and tested the boys' blood. He also did neurological evaluations on boys and conducted electroencephalography studies of their brain wave patterns. He gave some electroconvulsive therapy, also known as shock therapy. Adults who willingly agree to participate in medical testing or clinical research must be informed about the nature of the tests or experiments, as well as their risks and benefits. Adults who participate in medical experiments also have the right to opt out at any time. To acknowledge their rights and consent, they must sign legal paperwork. But the boys at Dozier were minors, so they were not legally able to provide consent for this experimentation, nor could they choose not to participate.

Larry E. Hogue was assigned to work in Dr. Souza's office, which was in a building called Pierce Hall. He describes his duty at the beginning of each day as preparing the "soup" and transferring it from the refrigerator to a large metal tub for that day's treatments. Hogue doesn't know exactly what was in the mixture, except for what he believed was ground meat of some kind. But he does remember the sight of its repulsive, orange-red color, as he handed the soup to boys in paper cups.

According to Hogue, soup making wasn't the only thing going on at Pierce Hall. Boys were also held in solitary confinement there for thirty days at a time in small rooms without toilets or sinks. Hogue recalls that some of these boys came to Pierce Hall after punishment at the white house.

Donald Fred Smith, for example, believes he spent a full ninety days in solitary, following a severe beating at the white house. He says that during that time, things were hazy because he was drugged. He remembers clearly having to drink Dr. Souza's so-called bone soup every afternoon before the evening meal. Smith believes Souza also hypnotized him and gave him shock treatments. Smith and other survivors of Dozier view themselves as guinea pigs for Souza's medical experimentation. Some Dozier survivors have searched for state records to document a valid Florida medical license for Souza during the years he was at the school. None has been found.

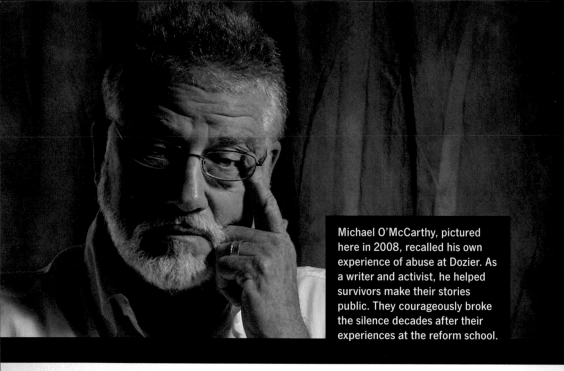

Chapter 5

MAKING THEMSELVES HEARD

I n the winter of 2006, Robert Straley had an unusual experience. Leafing through the newspaper, he read about the death of fourteen-year-old Martin Lee Anderson. Anderson was alleged to have died during a mandatory run at a boot camp–style youth detention facility in January that year. Surveillance footage later showed that after the teen had collapsed from exhaustion, several guards punched, kicked, and knelt on him as he lay on the ground. While reading the account, Straley suddenly experienced a flood of painful memories, choking him with fear for the next two days. Later, on the phone with a friend, Straley found himself unloading a string of horrific stories about his days at Dozier—for the first time in his life. His friend was shocked and told Straley that he could not keep the terrible secrets hidden anymore.

So Straley began searching the internet for information about Dozier. Online he ran across Roger Dean Kiser's accounts of the terrible events he had experienced at the school. Straley contacted Kiser, who responded and told him that other survivors had also seen his internet piece and reached out to him. In the following months, Straley and Kiser worked together by phone and email to collect as much information about Dozier as they could from state archives and newspaper reports. During their research, both men were struck by Dozier's lengthy history of inspections documenting horrible conditions at the school, all the way back to the early twentieth century. Yet, Florida officials appeared to have done little or nothing about it. Also nagging at Straley and Kiser was the fact that the school was still open. They worried that abuses might still be happening. They were.

With the floodgate of memories opened, Straley knew his post-Dozier nightmares and anxiety wouldn't go away unless he sought justice. Having found Kiser, Straley also knew he wasn't alone in seeking the truth.

In 2008 Kiser and Straley reached out to filmmaker, writer, and civil rights activist Michael O'McCarthy. O'McCarthy was a fellow Florida man known for his work to raise awareness of the Rosewood Massacre in Rosewood, Florida. In 1923 a race riot had culminated in the destruction of the small town. White citizens from a nearby town had murdered most of Rosewood's residents, who were black. After the massacre, neither local nor state law enforcement arrested any of the white citizens who had attacked Rosewood. During the early 1990s, O'McCarthy had investigated and written about Rosewood. Intending to produce a film about the incident, he had also pushed to find any survivors or their relatives and help them seek justice.

Because of O'McCarthy's activism, Straley hoped he would help seek justice for Dozier survivors. Straley emailed O'McCarthy, writing, "Help us expose the horrors of a place called 'The White House,' where hundreds of boys were raped, flogged and perhaps even murdered. Help us put an end to Florida's most shameful secret. . . . Can you do for us what you did for Rosewood?" When O'McCarthy read Straley's message, he was momentarily stunned. O'McCarthy had also been at Dozier as a teen, in the late 1950s, and had suffered brutally. It took O'McCarthy several days to work up the strength to call Straley.

When the two men finally spoke, they decided to create a website inviting other survivors of Dozier to get in touch. They realized additional stories from other former prisoners were needed to help confirm and build a strong legal case for what they themselves knew to be true from personal experience. Accounts began to funnel in from survivors and family members. These included the adult children of men who had been at Dozier but had never discussed their experiences in detail, or at all. After reading the online accounts of other survivors, the adult children of some understood why their fathers had been distant, moody, or unable to show them fatherly love. At about this same time, Straley and Kiser also got in touch with numerous media outlets, hoping that newspapers or television stations would pick up the story. A few did, and the movement to expose the horrors at Dozier began to gain momentum.

FINDING AN ADVOCATE

To be able to make a solid case, O'McCarthy knew the school survivors had to persuade someone in authority to listen to their story. O'McCarthy settled on Gustavo (Gus) Barreiro, a new employee at the Florida Department of Juvenile Justice. Barreiro was a Cuban immigrant who had come to Miami, Florida, in 1961, when he was two. While a sophomore at a Wisconsin college, Barreiro had written a paper in a criminal justice class about providing male role models for

Former congressional representative Gus Barreiro was a key advocate in pushing for justice for the Dozier survivors. He worked for the Florida Department of Juvenile Justice in 2008, when a group of survivors asked for his help.

delinquent boys. The paper influenced his professor to seek money to launch what became the Wisconsin Living Learning Center for boys with behavioral issues. At the urging of his professor, nineteen-year-old Barreiro opened the center and ran it for nine years.

In 1989 Barreiro moved back to Florida, where he continued his work as an advocate for children. He served four terms in the Florida House of Representatives, from 1998 through 2006. Among his more high-profile roles, Barreiro had chaired the legislature's special committee to investigate the Martin Lee Anderson case. This was the same young man whose death in custody had sparked Straley's determination to expose the wrongs at Dozier. In 2006 Barreiro was instrumental in passing Florida's Martin Lee Anderson Act. The law eliminated the boot camp–style detention facilities in the state. When Barreiro agreed to help O'McCarthy and Straley, the men of Dozier found one of their first champions.

BARREIRO'S MISSION

A few days after O'McCarthy's call, Barreiro received an unexpected assignment from the Florida Department of Juvenile Justice. To his surprise, he was asked to visit the Dozier School to investigate

Making Themselves Heard

Technological Witnesses

In 1967 the State of Florida banned corporal (physical) punishment at reform schools such as Dozier. Yet, as late as 1980, Dozier was still shackling boys and hog-tying them (tying wrists and ankles together as one, typically behind the victim's back) as a form of discipline.

Decades later, in 2007, a Dozier guard brutalized eighteen-year-old inmate Justin Caldwell, repeatedly bashing the young man's head into the concrete floor. The guard left Caldwell, who was bleeding from his forehead and later lost consciousness, on the floor for thirty minutes. Outraged, Caldwell's father contacted the FBI to investigate. Based on the investigation that followed, the Florida Department of Juvenile Justice fired the guard. The department eventually also fired the school's superintendent, who had five other confirmed cases of abuse under his leadership at the school. Many more cases were alleged to have taken place.

How were investigators able to confirm abuse at Dozier in the twenty-first century, when they had not been able to do so in earlier decades? Through the school's technological witnesses—surveillance cameras on campus. Three cameras had captured the attack on Caldwell, and with that evidence, there was no denying the guard's abuse.

allegations that guards were abusive to the inmates. This assignment was not a complete coincidence, since the department knew that, based on Straley and Kiser's outreach, news stories about Dozier were beginning to circulate. Other recent complaints about the school were coming to light as well. One was the abuse of Justin Caldwell in 2007, whose father was so enraged he had contacted the FBI about Dozier.

Barreiro was in the right place at the right time. He had the skills and position to help the growing group of survivors, who had come to be known as the White House Boys. Barreiro left for Dozier on the same day he got the assignment. He decided to start his mission by first going into Marianna to speak with people about what they knew or suspected of Dozier. He learned that most townspeople were well aware of the history of brutality at the school. Many of them had worked there in the past but had turned a blind eye. Once he was at Dozier itself, the staff was very helpful. They showed Barreiro everything he asked to see, from records to buildings to the inside of the infamous white house. Barreiro spent several days collecting information at Dozier before returning to his office in Miami.

Following his trip to Marianna, Barreiro suggested that O'McCarthy call *Miami Herald* newspaper reporter Carol Marbin Miller. As an investigative journalist, Marbin Miller's focus was on social services in Florida. She covered stories about people with disabilities, children, the elderly, and youth in the juvenile justice system. Marbin Miller and Barreiro knew each other from working together on cases of young people who had been abused and had even died while in Florida juvenile detention facilities. So O'McCarthy

Carol Marbin Miller is an award-winning investigative journalist with the *Miami Herald* newspaper. She specializes in juvenile justice and other human rights issues. In 2008 her reporting on abuses at Dozier broke the story and brought it to the attention of a wide audience.

called Marbin Miller in May 2008 and told her what he knew about Dozier. She took the next step and began to follow up on his story.

Meanwhile, Barreiro returned to Marianna to continue his investigation. He ate with and talked to the inmates at Dozier, witnessing some of the harsh behavior of guards. Barreiro came to recognize that most of the employees had very little training. They treated their work as simply a way to earn a living, not as service to help the boys in their care. Barreiro also visited the Jackson County Correctional Facility. It had been built in 1991 on what had been the old north campus of Dozier, where the school's black students once lived. It was there that Barreiro first learned of a cemetery in the woods on property that was once part of Dozier. That land had since become part of the Jackson County Correctional Facility. At Barreiro's request, correctional officials agreed to take him there.

In a clearing in the woods, Barreiro saw thirty-one white metal crosses laid out in neat rows. He took photos with his cell phone, not knowing if the graves could have any connection to the Dozier stories O'McCarthy and Straley had told him. The Jackson County correctional staff had no details about the cemetery. And Barreiro found that although the Dozier landscape crew cut the grass there, the Dozier superintendent wasn't even aware the cemetery existed. Barreiro called Marbin Miller to tell her of his discovery.

Barreiro then turned to a coworker at the Florida Department of Juvenile Justice. He told him about the White House Boys and about O'McCarthy's work on their behalf. He told him that the men were talking publicly about the abuse at Dozier. He pointed out that the stories were all similar—and that he had corroboration from many of the townspeople in Marianna. And he explained that the White House Boys wanted the State of Florida to come clean about the appalling history of abuse at Dozier. He made it clear the men wanted to hold the perpetrators accountable for their crimes, at least those who were still living. And the White House Boys wanted to visit the school as a way to try to heal the wounds of the past. Barreiro pointed out to his coworker the importance of getting in front of the story. He knew it was soon going to be scathing, front-page news. If handled well, the department's actions could make the agency look like the champions of the White House Boys—and not as if they were trying to cover up the abuse and protect the perpetrators.

The coworker believed Barreiro's approach was sound and helped put the ideas before their supervisors. Not only did the Florida Department of Juvenile Justice agree to Barreiro's plan; they chose him to organize and attend the visit the White House Boys would make to Dozier. Barreiro's supervisors knew that Marbin Miller was investigating the story too. Barreiro suggested that they also invite her to accompany the men to Dozier and to document how the department was trying to help the cause. October 21, 2008, was set as the date the White House Boys would travel to Marianna to face the past.

SEALING OF THE WHITE HOUSE

Meanwhile, based on a series of videotaped interviews Marbin Miller had conducted with several Dozier survivors—including Robert Straley, Roger Dean Kiser, and Michael O'McCarthy—she produced a newspaper story for the *Miami Herald*. It ran in the paper's Sunday edition on October 19, 2008. The story's release date was planned to coincide with the White House Boys' visit to the school two days later. The Florida Department of Juvenile Justice had scheduled the gathering and prepared a ceremony and plaque to be revealed at the event. The gathering was to be an official closing of the white house torture chamber. Marbin Miller's newspaper story was shocking. However, the timing left little chance for much reaction from the public or further investigation by other news outlets prior to the ceremony.

On Tuesday, October 21, 2008, as Associated Press and CNN News cameras filmed, five survivors—Dick Colon, Bill Haynes,

Gathering the Stories

Marbin Miller began conducting videotaped interviews with the White House Boys in 2008. From those stories, she wrote the October 2008 newspaper story—"A Painful Reunion at School of Horror"—that awoke the public to decades of abuse at Dozier. But Marbin Miller's account was not actually the first. O'McCarthy likely wrote the earliest published account about Dozier in 1980 in a collection of stories about life in the American South. Roger Dean Kiser had also been putting narratives of his Dozier experiences on his own websites since the 1980s. In the late 1990s, through a website designed to reconnect old classmates, Kiser had found other men who had attended Dozier. That was the start of the movement to unite survivors.

The work that Marbin Miller and Barreiro did together pushed the survivors' accounts into the limelight. From there, media coverage led to a public outcry and ongoing efforts to learn the truth of what happened at Dozier.

Roger Dean Kiser, Michael O'McCarthy, and Robert Straley—stood in front of the white house on the south side of Dozier's campus. They were there for the unveiling and dedication of the plaque. The plaque read, "In memory of the children who passed these doors, we acknowledge their tribulations and offer our hope that they have found some measure of peace. May this building stand as a reminder of the need to remain vigilant in protecting our children as we help them to seek a brighter future. Moreover, we offer the reassurance that we are dedicated to serving and protecting the youth who enter this campus, and helping them to transform their lives." At the bottom of the plaque was a signature line, reading, "The White House, Officially Sealed by the Florida Department of Juvenile Justice, October 21, 2008."

At the ceremony, each of the five men spoke about his experiences at Dozier. They told their stories to a crowd of about fifty. Some in the audience were from the governor's office and the press, while others were Dozier staff. The stories of horror and suffering were similar. Haynes, for example, relayed that he still bears both emotional and physical scars from his abuse at the school. He told the crowd that he had served in the Vietnam War in the 1960s, went on to a career as a corrections officer, and earned a college degree. In his three decades as a guard for the Alabama Department of Corrections, Haynes said he never once had to lay a hand on a prisoner, even those serving time for murder and rape. So why, he asked, did the Dozier staff believe it was necessary to so brutally beat the young boys in their care?

The plaque was then unveiled, and the crowd watched as the five survivors helped plant a tree in memory of the boys who had suffered at Dozier. Kiser spoke, saying, "Today, almost fifty years later, I now stand before you and I am still not sure if this building will ever allow me to smile. But that's not the worst of it all. A secret inner hatred of society and a fear of my fellowman will forever be instilled and kept secretly hidden deep inside me because of this white house building, the Florida Industrial School for Boys at Marianna, Dr. Robert Currie, Mr. Hatton and Mr. Troy Tidwell. . . . I stand here today in remembrance of all the boys who were beaten, raped, and abused by this facility."

Before the white house was officially sealed, the five attending survivors toured the building. The press photographed them, and Dozier staff hosted lunch for the ceremony's attendees. Kiser returned to the white house later that day and took an extensive series of photos to document the house of horrors before the state sealed it up, like a tomb.

Before they left, Straley and Barreiro searched for the place the Dozier boys had called the "rape room." They finally found the underground room at the back of the school. There, Straley had been sexually abused by an unknown man forty-five years earlier. Straley later described his feelings as he "stood silently in the doorway, remembering that night, so many years ago, when he had been trapped under the anonymous man, a young innocent, wondering what he had done that was bad enough to deserve such a terrible fate. If he had had a choice then, he thought he probably would have chosen death over what happened to him in that room. There had been so many nights after that when he wished he was dead. Finally, he knew why."

As the event neared its close, the Dozier survivors and the press made their way to what had been the north side of the Dozier campus. The nearby areas that had once been agricultural fields were overgrown and wooded. Abandoned buildings, covered in kudzu vines, still contained dilapidated bedframes and other furniture. The group walked to the clearing in the woods with its thirty-one nameless crosses. There, the survivors paid their respects to the boys who had not gotten out, whose lives had ended so tragically and prematurely at Dozier.

John Bonner (above) was a member of the Black Boys at Dozier Reform School support group. Some of those men visited the school in 2013 to speak about and reflect upon their experiences as boys at the institution. This photo was taken in one of the school dormitories.

THE "BLACK BOYS AT DOZIER"

A few years later, another group of Dozier survivors began to organize. They called themselves the Black Boys at Dozier Reform School. Like the White House Boys, they, too, had stories to tell. They, too, wanted a chance to revisit the school. So in August 2013, several of the men made their return, including John Bonner, Johnny Lee Gaddy, Arthur Huntly, and his brother Richard Huntly. Antoinette Harrell, a historian and author specializing in slavery, had helped them with researching and telling their stories.

While revisiting Dozier that summer day, each of the Black Boys at Dozier gave remarks to the assembled media and other invited guests. Gaddy explained that he and the other boys had not known how close the school was to Marianna. Being at Dozier as a young child had felt like being in a completely separate world. John Bonner said, "This school destroyed the lives of many boys, black and white. I am back today seeking justice and closure."

Some Dozier survivors alleged that staff occasionally killed inmates and buried their bodies at the small cemetery on campus. Investigations ultimately led to the excavations of the cemetery beginning in 2013.

Chapter 6

CLOSED WITHOUT CLOSURE

In December 2008, shortly after the White House Boys visited Dozier, Florida governor Charlie Crist called for the Florida Department of Law Enforcement (FDLE) to conduct two separate but overlapping investigations into Dozier. One team was to investigate the Dozier cemetery regarding the allegations of deaths at the school. A second group of law enforcement officials would handle the allegations of physical and sexual abuse that survivors had brought forward.

THE DEAD AT DOZIER

The FDLE cemetery investigation had two goals. One was to figure out how many graves were at Dozier. The other was to look for documents that would explain the cause and manner of those deaths at Dozier. Because the cemetery was so old, the team had trouble locating written records. The dormitory fire in 1914, for example, had destroyed some documents. And school staff had periodically cleaned out old files to make room for newer ones.

The paperwork that the FDLE team did find was badly damaged by water and mold. And in many cases, the team couldn't determine the accuracy of the documents. Authors weren't listed, which made it impossible to know whether the records were actually written by Dozier authorities. So the team turned to secondary sources to confirm as many burials as they could. The Dozier School newspaper, the *Yellow Jacket*, described a couple of funerals at the school. School reports and the local newspaper documented other Dozier burials.

Altogether, the FDLE team found records related to the cemetery's thirty-one known graves. Ten held the remains of people who had died in the 1914 dormitory fire. The other twenty-one burials took place between 1919 and 1952. The graves included burials of students and staff. Official death certificates were legally required in Florida beginning in 1899. But most counties in Florida did not produce official death certificates until after about 1917. And not until 1920 did the State of Florida require a physician to certify a death. So the team was not able to figure out the cause of each death. Among those that did have an explanation were these:

- 1 accidental drowning
- 1 boy who died after falling off a mule
- 1 boy who died having his tonsils removed
- 1 death from flu in a 1932 flu outbreak
- 2 deaths from tuberculosis

- 2 deaths from kidney ailments
- 6 deaths from pneumonia
- 1 death from a head injury during a fight with other students

The cemetery investigative team found records for another fifty students and employees who had died at the school but were buried elsewhere. Most died from disease, such as the flu, malaria, pneumonia, blood poisoning, cancer, and one heart attack. Several deaths were the result of accidents. These included drownings, a fire-related death, and two other deaths connected to auto accidents. One boy was strangled to death by a fellow student. Another boy had escaped Dozier, had stolen a car, and was later shot about 200 miles (322 km) away by a deputy sheriff.

THE FDLE DOZIER CEMETERY REPORT

In May 2009, the FDLE compiled a report on its cemetery investigation to sum up what it had been able to figure out. Disappointing to many, the report concluded, "During the course of the investigation it was determined that neither the School nor its staff made any attempt to conceal any student deaths. Furthermore, no evidence or information was discovered which indicated that any staff member was responsible for any student deaths at the School. . . . The investigation pertaining to the School's Cemetery will be closed due to lack of evidence as defined by Florida Statutes."

The FDLE cemetery report clarified that the team had based its investigation only on written records and a surface examination of the location, not by digging or scientific testing at the cemetery. It pointed out that the thirty-one crosses in the Dozier burial site were not meant to mark the exact positions of graves. So, to try to locate and exhume (dig up) specific graves would be difficult. The report also clarified that the team had not found cemetery records that matched names to precise locations in the graveyard. Furthermore, the FDLE found that part of the cemetery had been destroyed through farmwork during the 1980s or 1990s.

In the end, the FDLE did not favor digging to search for graves, believing that doing so would destroy their contents. The condition of the remains would likely not allow for positive identification of the individuals in the graves, since they had been in the ground for so long. The FDLE couldn't find information about the types of caskets used or whether remains had been embalmed or not. And the report pointed out that matching genetic material (deoxyribonucleic acid, or DNA) from any buried remains with the DNA from family members could be quite difficult. That would require locating living family members of boys who had been dead, in some cases, for nearly a century. Lastly, the report cautioned that Florida citizens and Dozier families might oppose digging up the remains for cultural or religious reasons. The report suggested that the team had done all it could to research the Dozier cemetery. It recommended that the State of Florida let the dead rest.

THAT WHICH DOESN'T KILL YOU

Governor Crist had also directed the FDLE to conduct a separate investigation into the allegations of abuse from Dozier survivors. These included many men who had been incarcerated at the school in the 1950s and 1960s. By their own accounts, they had been beaten, sexually abused, or both. The FDLE was instructed to find out if crimes took place and, if so, who broke the law and could therefore be held responsible.

Publicity from the October 2008 ceremony to seal the notorious Dozier white house had brought about one hundred people forward. Some were men who had previously been held at the school. Others were family members of former inmates at Dozier. Authorities interviewed these individuals, either in person or by phone. Some of the men said they had been abused. A subset of them claimed they had needed medical treatment following a beating. Others had never been abused but indicated they had observed boys who had been physically injured at the white house. Some former students asserted that Dozier staff had sexually abused them. A few former Dozier students said the discipline at the school had helped turn their lives around.

The FDLE interviews revealed similarities in the men's stories. Those who described discipline at the white house often called the experience a beating (not a spanking). They remembered that the implement was a leather strap, about 18 inches (46 cm) long and about 4 inches (10 cm) wide. Not all the survivors agreed about whether the strap had a strip of sheet metal between the two layers of leather. The men used similar language, however, about having to hold the top rail of the cot and stay facedown. They remembered that if they did not cooperate, the predetermined number of blows would start over. Many could list the names of the men they believed had beaten them. Some told of other boys enlisted to help hold them down. Some recalled the beating to be so violent that they were struck on the back or the legs rather than on the buttocks.

The FDLE also interviewed former Dozier supervisor William Mitchell and former superintendent Lenox Williams. Both told authorities they did use a strap of those dimensions for discipline, but it did not contain a sheet-metal insert. Williams, who was an employee from 1960 to 1983, said the "spankings" were a last resort. He said they were mostly related to escape attempts or physical violence against other students. He stated that no boy ever got more than a dozen hits and that another adult was always present as a witness. Mitchell, who worked at the school for almost forty years, between 1959 and 1996, reported even fewer blows. He said that students typically received five to ten blows and that he never saw any physical injuries related to the spanking punishment.

The investigators also interviewed five men who had been cottage fathers at Dozier. Three of the five were never present at a spanking but sometimes had to document the results. Two of those three said they witnessed welts and redness on students' buttocks, but nothing severe. The third described seeing blood on a boy's pants after a trip to the white house. He believed that the punishments there rose to the level of abuse. Two of the cottage fathers had been present at spankings. One attended a single event and said the result was bruising. The other stated he witnessed multiple spankings. In his opinion, the discipline went to an extreme level, in the range of twenty to forty hits with the strap. This man said the implement did not contain metal and these spankings were simply the prescribed form of punishment. He was not aware of anyone being bloodied or needing medical treatment after a trip to the white house.

The FDLE investigation into abuse also included personal accounts from four of the founding members of the organization called the White House Boys: Dick Colon, Roger Dean Kiser, Michael O'McCarthy, and Robert Straley. These men were all at Dozier for varying periods of time between 1957 and 1964. The FDLE gathered the names of the staff members the men believed had terrorized or physically abused them as boys. They included psychologist Robert Currie and school administrators Robert Hatton and Troy Tidwell. The number of times each survivor claimed to have been sent to the white house as a boy ranged from one (O'McCarthy, who was at the school for nine months) to eleven (Colon, who was at Dozier for more than two years). The men said that the approximate number of lashes on each occasion ranged from a low of twenty-five to a high of fifty.

In the course of their investigation, the FDLE also visited the white house. Crime scene technicians examined the building for physical evidence potentially related to any crimes committed there. They broke the seals that were put in place in October 2008 during the press event. Photos the survivors had taken in 2008 showed a dilapidated structure with what appeared to be red handprints smeared down some of the walls. Crime scene investigators tested some interior surfaces for bloodstains, using the chemical phenolphthalein. Even if blood is not visible, phenolphthalein will turn bright pink when it reacts with the hemoglobin in blood. The investigators especially focused on the two small rooms that survivors said were used for discipline, one for white students and the other for black. Investigators sampled two walls in each room, and negative test results suggested no blood present. They also checked areas in the hallway and the entry room and found no evidence of bloodstains. (Blood residue can last longer than fifty years under certain conditions.)

The FDLE's report on the abuse investigation was released in January 2010. It indicates that the FDLE could not substantiate (verify) allegations by Straley and others regarding sexual abuse at Dozier. All the same, several names came up during the interviews with survivors. They included psychologist Robert Currie, whom several survivors accused of sexual harassment, inappropriate touching, and other sex acts, and administrator Troy Tidwell. The FDLE report confirmed that, according to former superintendent Lenox Williams, Currie had been fired from the school on charges of inappropriate conduct. Currie died in 2000. Former superintendent Arthur Dozier and former director Robert Hatton, whose names frequently came up in the accounts of severe beatings, were also dead.

The FDLE was also unable to verify Colon's and Kiser's accounts of the on-campus death of a boy they claim had been tumbled like laundry in a clothes dryer. The investigators dismissed the incident due to inconsistencies between the men's stories and within their sworn testimonies. Authorities specifically pointed to differences in Kiser's written accounts of the laundry room incident in published sources.

The FDLE concluded it could neither support nor deny any allegations of physical or sexual abuse at Dozier. It found no blood or other evidence for injuries at the white house. And even though the FDLE interviews detailed brutal beatings at the white house, the report emphasized that none of the men had any permanent scars on their bodies from these "spankings." The FDLE did not address the psychological scars that often remain with victims of abuse for a lifetime.

Outraged by the report's conclusions, Roger Dean Kiser said on his website, "This has to be the most bogus investigation in the history of the State of Florida. The fox guarding the henhouse, blood on his mouth and paws, is asked to determine if he is or is not guilty. What other outcome did we expect?"

THE ONE-ARMED MAN

In January 2009, a few short months after the news of the horrors at Dozier first went public, four Dozier survivors and their families filed a class action lawsuit (a legal claim created by and on behalf of a group of people). The lawsuit charged four Florida state agencies—the Department of Corrections, the Department of Juvenile Justice, the Department of Children and Family Services, and the Department of Agriculture—and a single individual, Troy Tidwell, for abuses at Dozier.

Of all the alleged abusers at Dozier, Troy Tidwell—the one-armed man—was the only one who was still alive at the time of the lawsuit. (He is still alive at the time of publication of this book.) Tidwell worked at the school from 1943 until 1982. In 2009 he was still living near the school.

As part of the lawsuit, the court ordered Tidwell brought in for questioning. Tidwell was eighty-five years old at this time, and he told the court that it was not always easy to remember details from so long ago. All the same, he claimed that because he was not a superintendent or a director at Dozier, he did not have the authority to order spankings. He could only carry them out or witness them. He admitted to doing both.

Tidwell said, "I spanked children when I was [at Dozier], when I was told to. . . . I didn't like the job spanking boys, but it wasn't my rule. I just did what I was told to do or asked to do. The years that I worked at that school I tried to be as fair as I could to those kids and I would want anybody working with mine in a school like that to be the same."

Tidwell confirmed what Superintendent Lenox Williams also reported during the FDLE interviews, which were going on around this same time: that most discipline was to punish escape attempts. Tidwell described the leather strap, which in his memory did not have a metal layer. He confirmed that staff did direct boys in the

Troy Tidwell, known to Dozier inmates as "the one-armed man," walks with a cane in May 2009 after testifying before the FDLE. Tidwell was named by hundreds of survivors as one of their abusers during the 1950s and 1960s. Due to the passage of time and lack of evidence, however, authorities were not able to prosecute him.

white house to lie facedown on the cot and hold the rails. Tidwell also admitted that, if necessary, staff called in other boys from the kitchen to restrain boys who resisted punishment. According to Tidwell, six was the usual number of blows for minor offenses, eight to ten for serious wrongdoing. He claimed that Dozier "spankings" were no worse than the ones he gave his own kids at home. They were not beatings, he said. Nor did he raise his arm any higher than his head to deliver a blow. Tidwell also said that he could not recall that any boy was ever bloodied. Nor did any boy ever need medical attention after a punishment session at the white house.

In the end, the lawsuit against Tidwell and the various Florida state agencies was dismissed in 2010. The judge ruled that if any crimes had been committed at Dozier, they were beyond the statute of limitations. In other words, the cases were too old to prosecute. But in February 2011, based on much more recent events that were coming to light at Dozier, two Florida legal services teams brought a case against Dozier to the Civil Rights Division of the US Department of Justice (DOJ). The lawsuit claimed civil rights violations against the Dozier School for Boys as violations of the Fourteenth Amendment to the US Constitution. Among the many provisions in that amendment are that incarcerated youth must be kept safe from harm.

The lawsuit named two current administrators of Dozier and the school's supervising organization, the Florida Department of Juvenile Justice. The lawsuit alleged that boys in the school's care were being physically abused through inappropriate use of force and physical restraints. And it alleged they were sometimes put in isolation for days or weeks at a time, without proper treatment.

In December of that year, the DOJ released a twenty-eight-page report condemning the actions at Dozier. The DOJ concluded that youth confined at the school had been "subjected to conditions that placed them at serious risk of avoidable harm in violation of their rights protected by the Constitution of the United States. During our investigation, we received credible reports of misconduct by staff members to youth within their custody." The report found excessive and unnecessary use of force and inappropriate confinement, including isolation. The DOJ also found a lack of adequate medical care as well as unsanitary and unsafe conditions that endangered the students. The report concluded that Dozier had failed to provide the rehabilitative services for which it was responsible.

However, the DOJ report of December 2011 did not make its conclusions from the historic accounts from the White House Boys or the Black Boys at Dozier. Nor did it pull from the FDLE interviews about abuses said to have occurred at the school from the 1950s through the 1970s. The official condemnation of Dozier came instead from the DOJ's investigations into the facility while it was still open in the twenty-first century. More than one hundred years after the school first opened its doors, and despite countless reports of mistreatment during that time, abuses were still taking place at Dozier.

With pressures mounting from all sides, the Florida Department of Juvenile Justice announced on May 26, 2011, that it planned to shut down the school. The official explanation was that Dozier was having financial troubles and could no longer afford to stay in business. After 111 years, Dozier was finally closed.

Erin Kimmerle is a biological and forensic anthropologist with experience working at mass grave sites. She led the University of South Florida excavation team at the Dozier cemetery.

Chapter 7
DIGGING FOR THE TRUTH

Among the most serious allegations of the Dozier survivors was that staff had intentionally murdered boys in their care. Although the FDLE report did not support those accounts, public pressure to conduct a forensic investigation of the cemetery mounted. After much discussion and debate, Florida officials decided to allow a group of scientists to explore the school's burial ground.

In 2012, one year after Dozier was officially shut down, authorities at the Historical Resources division of the Florida Department of

Environmental Protection issued a permit to researchers with the University of South Florida (USF) in Tampa. The permit gave USF permission to survey and map the Dozier cemetery. The USF project would also examine any available records to verify that the thirty-one metal crosses at Dozier actually marked a burial ground. If the records did so, the project would attempt to confirm how many graves were there. When the USF team finished its initial examination in December of 2012, it estimated that a minimum of fifty people had been buried at the site.

In March 2013, the Florida attorney general, Pam Bondi, asked a state court to allow researchers to dig at the Dozier cemetery. Bondi said, "The deaths that occurred at Dozier School for Boys in Marianna are cloaked in mystery, and the surviving family members deserve a thorough examination of the site. . . . I am committed to doing everything within my power to support investigative efforts to help resolve unanswered questions and bring closure to the families who lost loved ones." On August 6, 2013, in a room packed with Dozier survivors and their supporters, the court approved Bondi's request for the dig. Some people applauded, while others wiped away tears.

During her time as Florida's attorney general, Pam Bondi pushed for support of the exhumations at Dozier.

UNIVERSITY OF SOUTH FLORIDA DIGS IN

Florida governor Rick Scott, his advisers, the Florida Department of Environmental Protection, and USF entered into an agreement. It would allow law enforcement agents, crime scene technicians, and the university's anthropologists, librarians, and students to more

Digging for the Truth

thoroughly research the Dozier cemetery and grounds. The team would continue the review of Dozier property and records, while others would conduct further scientific testing. Most importantly, the team had the legal permissions to exhume graves and attempt to identify the dead. These USF experts directed the project:

- Erin Kimmerle, biological and forensic anthropologist, and the team's leader. Biological anthropologists investigate human beings using aspects of their physical makeup. Forensic anthropologists apply their knowledge of skeletal biology to legal matters.
- Richard Estabrook, archaeologist. Archaeologists are anthropologists who study humans and their culture through the material artifacts they leave behind. These artifacts can include human remains.
- Antoinette Jackson, cultural and historical anthropologist. Cultural anthropologists are experts in human customs and societies and how those aspects of culture develop and change over time.
- E. Christian Wells, environmental anthropologist. Environmental anthropologists study how humans interact with the world around them. These surroundings include ecology, climate, natural resources, plants and animals, and other features of the environment.

Kimmerle was chosen to lead the project because she had previous experience in forensic anthropology dedicated to civil rights and justice. She had worked with the United Nations (UN). This international organization is devoted to humanitarian issues such as protecting

Antoinette Jackson served as the cultural and historical anthropologist on the University of South Florida team. She and others helped locate and gather documents, images, and interviews that could reveal aspects of Dozier history.

human rights and ensuring peace around the globe. Kimmerle's work with the UN International Criminal Tribunal for the former Yugoslavia involved exhuming and identifying the bodies of thousands of victims of war crimes in the Yugoslavian civil war in southeastern Europe in the 1990s. Other members of the Dozier team also had experience in similar projects involving the search for justice.

Kimmerle spoke about the importance of the Dozier project. She said, "All through history, as this school was in operation, it was a closed facility. . . . The public has a lot of questions. . . . I think it's really good to be transparent, and to be open, and to share the information that we've been able to learn through our research. And just to share that history, it is a collective history. . . . Even though these events are in the past—for the people affected, the families and the victims—it's current, it's not historical, it's today, and I hope this provides the resolution and information that they're looking for."

To establish written documentation, the USF team studied newspapers and other available primary-source documents. They gathered court paperwork, death certificates, and Dozier attendance

Digging for the Truth

records. They discovered that close to one hundred boys between the ages of six and eighteen had died at Dozier between 1900 and 1973. Forty-five of those boys were buried at Dozier, and another thirty-one were buried elsewhere. The USF team could not determine where another twenty-two listed boys had been buried.

The USF group also turned to historical archives for maps and photos of the Dozier property. They interviewed former Dozier employees and others who might have had personal memories of the cemetery and related topics. The USF team also interviewed the families of missing boys who had once been at Dozier. The group also looked at genealogy records to look for relatives of people they believed had been buried at Dozier. All of this information would be useful for making comparisons to the human remains that the exhumation would eventually recover at Dozier.

THE HALLOWED GROUND

Originally called Cedar Hill, the Dozier cemetery was later known as the Boot Hill Cemetery or Boot Hill Burying Ground. The cemetery was created early in the school's history on the black side of the property (the north end). It sat in a clearing next to a dump, where the school burned its trash. The USF researchers found that in the early 1960s, the Dozier Boy Scout troop had marked the site with thirty-one cement crosses. (The superintendent at the time assumed thirty-one sets of remains had been buried at the site. He did not know exactly where.) The crosses were large—48 inches (122 cm) tall, each with an 18-inch (46 cm) crossbar—and reinforced by steel rebar (rods). In 1996 the school took down the cement crosses, replacing them with new crosses made out of metal pipe. For a protective fence around the site, the school put up metal poles attached to a thick wire. Like the earlier markers, the pipe crosses were meant as a memorial.

To prepare for exhuming bodies, the USF team removed plant overgrowth in the cemetery. Then they used ground-penetrating radar to look below the surface of the burial ground. Like other forms of radar, the technology sends out electromagnetic pulses, which come back to the source equipment (which includes a computer) to build an image of what the radar "sees." Experts interpreted the images, looking for anything out of the ordinary in the ground, including unexpected structures or obvious disturbances in the soil. They used pin flags to mark areas where the radar showed irregularities. From the pin flags, the anthropologists would create a map of the Dozier burial grounds and other places where bodies might have been buried. (The USF team found no additional gravesites in distant locations on Dozier property.)

For the pin flag and overall site mapping, the USF crew used a total station surveying system. This computerized surveying equipment measures geographic data points, such as distances and angles.

The University of South Florida team conducted ground-penetrating radar surveys in 2012 to produce this map for locating possible graves in the Dozier campus cemetery. The technology shows disturbances in the soil, seen here by differences in colors.

Digging for the Truth

The system uses the survey data to create a detailed map. The crew also took notes and photos at all stages.

The next step was to dig test zones. The zones would help outline the cemetery margins. They would also show the stratigraphy (layering) of the soil. USF anthropologists would use that information to compare undisturbed and disturbed areas of the cemetery. Finally, the USF team leaders directed the careful and systematic removal of the surface layers of soil with backhoes and other earth-moving equipment. When the top layer of soil is removed at a burial site, archaeologists can often see the outlines of grave shafts (the column-shaped excavations in which burials take place). They are easy to see because the consistency and color of the undisturbed soil around the grave shaft is not the same as the soil that was removed, mixed up, and put back in the grave shaft after the burial.

GRAVE MATTERS

Exhumation of human remains began. During the excavation process, a tentlike cover protected the burial sites from weather and sunlight. In

Off the Beaten Path

The USF exhumation project followed up on allegations of additional Dozier burials at sites other than Boot Hill Cemetery. These claims included burials on the south campus (the former white side). The USF team used ground-penetrating radar at thirty-three different locations covering about 3 acres (1.2 ha) on the south campus. They probed soil and dug test pits but found no additional burials outside the general vicinity of the cemetery.

The team also excavated the site of the 1914 dormitory fire. They recovered some bone fragments that were possibly of human origin but were too small or too damaged for further analysis. After their work was done, the crew filled in all disturbances in and outside the cemetery. Since then fast-growing vegetation has mostly taken over the areas of exhumation.

Excavations began with earth-moving equipment. Ultimately, much of the work was done by hand using shovels and trowels. Individuals from many agencies joined the process, including students from the University of South Florida.

the evening, the team put a tarp over the graves that were being worked on. Officials guarded the site overnight.

Initially, machine excavators removed soil from each grave until coffin hardware or the wood from the top of a casket appeared. Then a team of two or three individuals stepped in to continue the excavation more carefully, digging by hand with shovels and trowels. As with most archaeological work, the Dozier burials were excavated in pedestal style. Workers left items in place, removing the soil above and around them, but not beneath them. As the team found coffins, skeletal remains, and artifacts, they carefully examined and photographed them in situ (in place). Then the archaeologists removed more soil in stages. They sifted the soil through screen mesh to look for small bones, buttons, coins, and any other artifacts that might have been buried with the individual or been in the grave for unrelated reasons. The team mapped and photographed each stage of the excavations and everything found there.

Detailed examination of historical records suggested the USF team would find thirty-four persons buried in the school cemetery, and not the original thirty-one represented by the metal crosses. However, the actual fieldwork discovered fifty-five graves containing fifty-one individuals. The team found that charred remains from the 1914 fire had been divided into multiple coffins, each in its own grave. Anthropological analysis of those graves actually showed that fewer people had been buried than the total number of burial containers. The team also found that the charred remains had been buried in different types of caskets. Some burned bones from the fire were in professionally built infant-sized caskets. Most remains in the cemetery, however, were in coffins that were apparently handmade, perhaps by Dozier staff or students. Of the fifty-five graves, only thirteen were within the clearing where the thirty-one crosses once stood. None of those were directly beneath any of the thirty-one markers, as would be expected if the crosses had been confidently matched to graves. The other forty-two burials were outside the mowed portion of the cemetery. They were found among the woods and brush or beneath the vehicle lane leading to the cemetery.

ANALYZING SKELETONS AND GRAVE GOODS

A team of forensic anthropologists examined and photographed the skeletal remains in the USF forensic anthropology laboratory. Staff at the medical examiner's office in Tampa took X-rays for review by forensic pathologists (medical doctors who specialize in disease, trauma, and poisons and the effects they have on the body). Their goal was to assess the likely age, sex, height, and ancestry of each person, if possible. They would also try to document any injuries or diseases they could see by studying each person's bones.

Dental disease was the most common condition anthropologists saw among the remains of the children buried at Dozier. Excluding the remains from the 1914 fire, 83 percent of the skeletal remains had at least one untreated cavity. One boy had seventeen cavities. Only one skull had metallic dental fillings. More than half of the boys' skeletons showed bone damage from serious ear infection. Many of these children lived before antibiotics were available. Some remains also showed evidence of malnutrition and growth problems typical of children who are not getting enough food or who have nutritional disturbances.

Forensic Anthropology

The science of anthropology, specifically biological or forensic anthropology, can provide information about a person's physical life and identity from their skeleton. Anthropological measurements and examination of bones help scientists estimate a person's age at death. Depending on that age, features such as the width and depth of the pelvis, the dimensions of joint surfaces, the shapes and sizes of various features in the skull, and other body regions can help determine if the person was most likely male or female. Observations and measurements of facial features and skull dimensions can also provide clues about a person's ancestral (racial) background. Other bone measurements can reveal approximately how tall the person stood during life. Some diseases and injuries leave specific marks in bone. So experts will examine remains for their state of health or possible cause of death.

Depending on the condition of the skeleton, anthropologists can create a biological profile of an individual. This may include that person's age, sex, race, and height. With this information, anthropologists, death investigators, and others work to figure out who the person might (or might not) be. Sometimes unique features in the skeleton or its teeth can be compared to existing records of missing people to make a positive identification. Scientists can also take samples of bone, teeth, or hair for DNA and other chemical testing. They will compare the results to information about people who are missing as they work to provide a name for the unknown victim.

Digging for the Truth

Experts in historic artifacts analyzed grave goods (items buried with a body). The experts divided the artifacts into three main classes: hardware such as nails, screws, and casket handles from the coffins; personal items, including clothing fasteners and items that may have been in the victims' pockets; and miscellaneous historic and more modern debris, including glass fragments from old soft drink bottles, used syringes, and medicine vials. The debris was likely from the dump or the different soils used to fill in the burials. The team recorded the precise positioning of each artifact relative to the grave where it was found. They washed and photographed all the items, which numbered in the thousands. The dates of objects such as casket hardware and coins were used to help figure out the approximate era in which an individual was buried.

Team members also took samples from the human remains for DNA testing. (The bone fragments from those who had died in the 1914 fire were too damaged to produce DNA profiles.) Nearly thirty family members of boys who had been at Dozier provided DNA reference samples to help with identification. All this information—from artifacts, the remains, and their DNA profiling—for each individual would then be compared to death certificates and other existing records. Matches would help establish the identity of the people buried at Dozier.

In January 2016, the USF team published its final report. Through DNA testing, the cemetery project had been able to positively identify seven individuals. The families of four of them later decided to rebury the remains at locations of their choice. Based on artifacts and other clues and testing, the USF team believed they could make presumptive identifications for fourteen more individuals. (For anthropologists "presumptive" refers to a possible identification based on biological and other consistencies with known historical information about the deceased, such as their sex and age. It is not based on factors unique to a single person, such as DNA, fingerprints, or dental evidence that scientists use to confirm positive identity.)

George Owen Smith

In August 2014, Erin Kimmerle and her USF team made the first positive identification of skeletal remains at Dozier: George Owen Smith. In 1940, when he was fourteen, Smith had been sentenced to Dozier for allegedly stealing a car. Just a couple of months later, officials notified Smith's mother that her son's decomposing body had been discovered, off campus, beneath the porch of a house in Marianna. The condition of his body made it difficult to know for certain how he had died. But the officials believed Smith may have died of pneumonia while hiding under the house.

Smith's mother knew that he had run away from the school once and that authorities had brought him back. She hadn't heard from him again for a while, so she wrote to the school to find out about her son's whereabouts. The school informed her that he had run away again and that they did not know where he was. The next day, in January 1941, Smith and her husband borrowed a car and traveled to the school with their daughter Ovell. It was then that Dozier officials explained that the boy's body had been found earlier that morning. Staff showed the family a fresh mound of dirt in the cemetery. This, staff told the couple, was their son's gravesite. It lay to the end of one of two rows of unmarked burials near the woods. The family always wondered if the grave actually contained George's body, and if so, how he died and why he was buried so quickly.

Many decades later, Smith's sister, former police officer Ovell Krell, learned of the USF project at Dozier. She volunteered to provide a DNA sample for comparison to any remains the team recovered. When she learned her DNA was a match to the DNA from one set of remains, Krell said, "I couldn't believe it after 73 and a half years of fighting and looking and hoping and praying, and I was searching for him, not only out of my love, but for a vow I made my mother and father on their death beds that I would find my brother if it's in my power . . . I would look 'til I died."

At the age of eighty-five, Krell had found her brother. She reburied his remains beside the graves of their parents.

Individuals Positively Identified Using DNA Testing

Name	Death year	Age	Reported ancestry	Listed cause of death
Loyd Dutton	1918	14	White	Unknown
Sam Morgan	1921	21	White	Unknown
Thomas Varnadoe	1934	13	White	Pneumonia
Grady Huff	1935	17	White	Kidney disease
Robert Stephens	1937	15	Colored	Stabbing
George Owen Smith	1941	14	White	Unknown, escapee
Earl Wilson	1944	12	Colored	Head injuries, beaten

Forensic scientists used DNA to positively identify seven of the people buried at Dozier. At the time these people died, "colored" was the accepted word for black people. Of the seven on this list, Sam Morgan was paroled to perform farm labor off campus grounds, was soon returned to the school, died, and was buried there. Robert Stephens was stabbed to death by another Dozier student, who was charged with his killing. At the time of his death, Earl Wilson was being held along with eight other boys in a tiny shed at Dozier as punishment. Four of those boys beat him to death and were later charged with his murder.

SEGREGATION, EVEN IN DEATH

The USF team studied the maps they had created of the placement of graves at the Dozier cemetery. Based on positive or tentatively identified remains in twenty-one of the graves, at least one expert thinks that the Dozier cemetery was probably segregated by race, at least for part of its history. Segregated cemeteries in the United States were common until the 1950s. At Dozier the graves of white individuals were clustered in the northwestern end of the cemetery (with the exception of the final cemetery burial of a black student in that same area). The graves of nonwhites were clustered in the southeastern portion of the cemetery. If more identifications are made, other graves could change the understanding of how race guided the placement of graves at the Dozier cemetery.

Presumptive Identifications

Name	Death year	Age	Reported ancestry	Listed cause of death
Bennett Evans	1914	Adult	White	Fire
Charles Evans	1914	Adult	White	Fire
Thomas Adkins	1918	12	Colored	Unknown
Lee Goolsby	1918	13	White	Unknown, escapee
George Grissam	1918	6	Colored	Unconscious, paroled
Willie Adkins	1918	13	Colored	Unknown
Wilbur Smith	circa 1918	10	Colored	Flu, reportedly
John H. Williams	1921	15	Colored	Accident
Schley Hunter	1922	16	White	Pneumonia/influenza
Richard Nelson	1935	12	Colored	Pneumonia/influenza
Robert Cato	1935	12	Colored	Pneumonia/influenza
Joshua Backey	1935	14	Colored	Blood poisoning
James Hammond	1936	14	Colored	Tuberculosis
Billey Jackson	1952	13	Colored	Kidney disease, escapee

By studying various documents and comparing them to the exhumed remains, anthropologists were able to come up with presumptive identifications for fourteen of the people buried at Dozier. Documents show that young George Grissam had been temporarily released to work as a houseboy off campus. He was returned to the school unconscious, died, and was buried there.

The USF team found that race impacted aspects of the records the school kept of its cemetery. For example, they noted that a boy's grave was three times more likely not to be listed in death records if he was black. In addition, nonwhites were more often not even named in death documents. Sometimes paperwork simply stated, "One unnamed colored boy died." Overall, about 25 percent of the individuals reported to have died at the school were white, and about 75 percent were black. This reflects the recorded school attendance by race over time: blacks greatly outnumbered whites during much of Dozier's history.

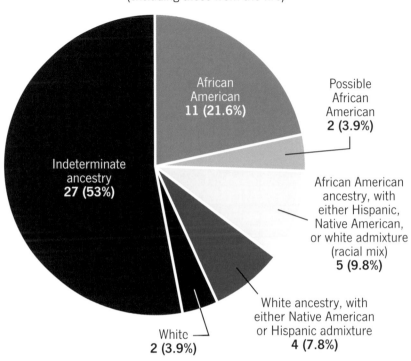

DOZIER GRAVES BY RACIAL ANCESTRY
Total number of single graves: **51**
(excluding those from the fire)

African American
11 (21.6%)

Possible African American
2 (3.9%)

Indeterminate ancestry
27 (53%)

African American ancestry, with either Hispanic, Native American, or white admixture (racial mix)
5 (9.8%)

White ancestry, with either Native American or Hispanic admixture
4 (7.8%)

White
2 (3.9%)

Source: *Report on the Investigation into the Deaths and Burials at the Former Arthur G. Dozier School for Boys in Marianna, Florida*, Forida Institute of Forensic Anthropology and Applied Science, University of South Florida, 2016

FACING DEATH

Of the fifty-one individuals buried in single graves, twelve (23.5 percent) were assessed as male. The sex of the remaining thirty-nine (76.5 percent) was listed as indeterminate. The skeletal traits that help experts determine sex were too damaged by environmental deterioration or were not yet developed at the time of the person's death. Sex differences in the skeleton are due to hormonal changes that occur during puberty, and some of these boys had not reached that stage in life. DNA testing can reveal the presence of the male Y chromosome throughout life. But most of the Dozier remains were

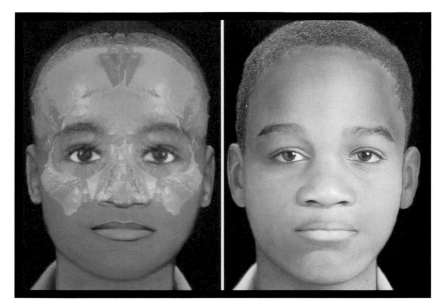

This is an artist's facial reconstruction from the skull in the grave known as Burial 36. The skeleton in that grave is that of an eight- to fourteen-year-old black male whose identity is not known. Only two of the exhumed skulls were complete enough to allow this facial reconstruction technique.

too degraded for experts to obtain a useful DNA sample. As for estimating the ages of the deceased, the bones of three individuals were too damaged to assess. Of the remaining forty-eight, the youngest (probably George Grissam) was estimated at six to ten years of age. The oldest of the students (Sam Morgan) was estimated at twenty to forty years of age; records in fact show that he was twenty-one when he died.

Two of the skulls were complete enough in their midface region to allow for a computerized facial reconstruction to show how they might have looked in life. To create the computerized facial approximations, forensic artists worked with the known or suspected sex, ancestry, and age of the victims from the anthropological analysis of their bones.

To do this, anthropologists first create a three-dimensional scan of the skull. This scan is input to a computer software program that uses images of the facial skeleton to digitally re-create how the person probably looked in life. The standards for how the software puts "flesh" back on the bones are based on scientifically established tissue depths in various areas of the face.

One reconstruction was that of a black boy estimated at eight to fourteen years of age when he died. He is known only as Burial 36 at this point. The age of the other boy, who was also black, is estimated at thirteen to fourteen and a half years of age. He is known only as Burial 13.

Investigators aren't always able to determine an absolute cause of death from skeletal remains. Many injuries and diseases do not leave a trace in bone. In addition, remains may be damaged as a result of their time in the ground. Acidic soils, root growth, and water drainage are some of the natural processes that can take a toll on buried remains over time. When bones are badly damaged, such as by the environment, their surfaces and other features that might show signs of disease or trauma (such as a fracture) can be worn away.

One grave (Burial 33) contained the skeleton of an individual the USF team presumptively identified as John Williams, a black teen between the ages of thirteen and seventeen. From DNA sampling, the team thought he could perhaps have also been of American Indian or Hispanic origin. They found a small ball of lead in the area of the grave where his upper left thigh or lower left abdominal region would have been. Firearms experts said the pellet's appearance, size, and weight resembled "triple aught" (000) buckshot. This type of large ammunition is used in shotguns for hunting and self-defense. Records show that a John Williams died in 1921 during an accident. But the firearms experts could not confirm that the pellet was in the boy's body when he died. If the identity of the boy is someday confirmed through a DNA match with relatives, they may be able to offer more information about the accident. But 1921 was a long time ago, and the likelihood that relatives are still living is remote. Finding living relatives is especially difficult when the dead, such as the young boys at Dozier, did not live long enough to have children. In cases like this, researchers will search instead for siblings, cousins, nieces, and nephews.

"DECADES OF DARKNESS CANNOT HIDE ALL THINGS"

None of the victims at Dozier had clear signs that demonstrated or even hinted that the school was responsible for their untimely deaths. Because the boys came to Dozier from different backgrounds and at various ages, even the illnesses and malnutrition they may have suffered cannot be definitively tied to the school. The USF investigation could not confirm neglect, abuse, or even specific causes of death from the remains of those buried at the school. Still, some of the Dozier survivors have not given up hope that their memories of abuse will one day be confirmed through scientific evidence. When USF released its exhumation report, survivor Robert Straley said, "These boys' lives were not lost in vain, for their stories changed the laws of Juvenile Justice in Florida, and their monument should be a shining reminder that decades of darkness cannot hide all things. May their many candles burn brightly, and may their candles be lit for the boys that may never be found. It is better to extend a hand, than raise a fist. Forgiveness is only for the strong."

John Due and his daughter Tananarive visited the Dozier cemetery in 2013. Their relative, Robert Stephens, was stabbed to death by another Dozier student in 1937. Stephens was among the seven young men whose remains were positively identified using DNA technology.

Chapter 8

"THE BONES STILL CRY OUT"

USF's final Dozier report was released in January 2016. In May 2016, Florida's state attorney announced that insufficient evidence and statutes of limitation meant that arrests or prosecutions related to the White House Boys, the Black Boys at Dozier, or any other survivors with allegations from the past were unlikely.

Meanwhile, survivors pushed for a public, formal apology from Florida lawmakers to recognize the suffering that had taken place at Dozier. And the next year, in April 2017, the survivors of the abuse received a formal apology from the Florida State Legislature. Both the state senate and its house of representatives were unanimous in their support of the apology. They invited survivors to a ceremony at which the apology was read aloud. At the ceremony, state senator Darryl Rouson stated, "This resolution on behalf of this Florida Senate commits to ensuring that the children of Florida are protected from this kind of abuse and violations of fundamental human decency." To the Dozier survivors at the ceremony, he added, "Through you, yet the living, the bones still cry out." Bill Price, one of the White House Boys who had worked to secure the apology, said, "We've been waiting on this for 10 years. It's something we have fought for 10 years. We do deserve an apology, and we will accept it."

In early 2018, former Dozier inmates and their advocates turned their efforts in another direction. Under a proposed new law, Dozier survivors who were at the school between 1940 and 1975, and who were willing to swear to enduring specific abuses, could be officially declared "victims of abuse." Doing so might give them additional legal rights and the potential for financial compensation for the personal damages they allege. But by March 2018, the bill had gone nowhere, and passage is unlikely.

STANDING UP FOR OTHERS

The Dozier survivors came together to share their stories and seek justice. So far, they have not received any financial settlements, and the lawsuits were not successful. However, the State of Florida did designate $1.2 million to build a memorial to the young men who lived and those who died at Dozier between 1900 and 1973. Plans are to erect a monument on the state capitol grounds in Tallahassee, rather than at the school. Some of the White House Boys do not want the memorial in Marianna, believing the town was complicit in the wrongdoings at Dozier. Some Marianna citizens do not want the memorial there because of the continued attention the monument would bring to the town. No date has been set for the completion of the monument.

In August 2018, the state made arrangements to rebury the bodies that were still unidentified. The charred remains from the 1914 fire would return to Dozier property. The additional unidentified remains will not be returned to the school, however. Local funeral director Art Kimbrough points out that many Marianna residents do not want the burials replaced there. They have what he calls "the anger of being painted as a town of torturers." Nor do Dozier survivors want their deceased "brothers" sent back to the school, a place of so much pain. So the unidentified remains will be transported to Tallahassee, Florida, to be buried in donated graves. If additional DNA testing produces more positive identifications, the state will pay to exhume those remains again and bury them at a site of the family's choosing.

The brotherhood of Dozier survivors continues to share grief and work toward healing. In April 2018, a group of survivors traveled to Dozier by bus for a tour and memorial service. Though the tour was private, some neighbors spoke out. Marianna resident Jack Hollis stated, "I just hope they get their closure." But Hollis, like some of the other residents of Marianna, wants the attention to end. He says, "It's like shame, you know, it's a big shame thing on [the town]."

Outsiders still wonder how abuse could happen for so long under state supervision and with the town nearby. Kimmerle sums up, "One thing you see with Dozier through its hundred years: It's not that there weren't investigations and people who knew what was happening, but the main institutional systems that were there that perpetuated the violence, that culture, were always left intact."

Michael O'McCarthy, who first published accounts of abuse at Dozier in 1980, died in 2010 without seeing any resolution. Robert Straley, O'McCarthy's partner in bringing the story to Gus Barreiro and Carol Marbin Miller, died in 2018. Bill Price, who helped secure the state's apology to victims, also died in 2018.

Breaking the Silence

The Dozier story of abuse, like so many other similar accounts, is complicated. It starts with abuse of power as adults in authority hurt vulnerable, powerless children or others in their care. Those in power often establish a confusing mix of trust and fear in their victims, who suffer in secrecy, silence, shame, and hopelessness. The perpetrators know they are doing wrong. They realize that disgrace will come down on them and the institution for which they work, should the truth come out. So they lie about their deeds or are silent.

Survivors of abuse pay a terrible price. Many have difficulty building and maintaining close relationships. They may turn to substance abuse to ease their suffering. They may have trouble holding down a job or may fall into a life of crime. All live with emotional trauma. Some are able to function despite their pain; others cannot.

In coming forward with their truth, the Dozier survivors broke their silence. In doing so, they shed light on shared experiences of torture, rape, and humiliation while they were at the Dozier School as young boys. Going public led to formal police investigations and an official exhumation project. Yet these efforts were unable to legally substantiate that the abuse actually took place. Remains were too degraded to provide reliable forensic evidence, and many of the victims and perpetrators are dead.

Without enough evidence to pursue legal justice, what did the men gain from coming forward with their stories? They gained back some of the dignity and potential that was taken from them as children. They also created a permanent record—through the news articles and books written about Dozier, the legal and scientific steps undertaken, and the public monument that will be built. Society can look to that record, recognize the pain these men suffered as boys, and better support other people who come forward about abuse. This has been true for similar cases of inhumanity that were made public, including neglect in orphanages and other care facilities; abuses in internment, detention, and concentration camps; and sexual abuse within the Catholic Church and other institutions. The efforts of those involved with exposing the horrors at Dozier break these silences and help ensure justice and increased protection for society's most vulnerable.

Time is running out for Dozier's survivors. No additional identifications have been made from the USF exhumations. In the final analysis, if boys were abused and killed by staff members and buried at Dozier, their remains have not been found. Time—and the earth—seem to have buried the school's secrets.

Richard Huntly, of the Black Boys at Dozier Reform School, has not given up supporting those, dead or alive, who suffered at the school. He concludes with a message of determination and hope:

> We're here for them. We will stand for them. We . . . are also looking for justice for all the boys who got caught up in that slave camp. We're here to try to help protect the rights of the boys that are still caught up in other similar reform school situations. Mariana was one of the worst places in the world—I see it now as a concentration camp. Irreparable damage was done to all of the boys that were there, getting no education and having nowhere to go. When they went back home, they were tagged, "that old boy from reformatory school." They had no friends. They had to make their own way. I think that resulted in many of those boys ending up in prison . . . because of the anger they had inside of them that the [school] beat into them, creating in them a lifestyle that could not fit in with normal society. . . . The State of Florida robbed us of our childhood, yet we overcame. You beat us and worked us like slaves, yet we endured it. When we were children, you took our freedom away for no reason other than for your greedy gain . . . but in the end, we will also win.

Source Notes

5   State of Florida, *The General Statutes of the State of Florida* (Saint Augustine, FL: Record, 1906), 1486.

7   State of Florida, 1487.

7   State of Florida.

8   State of Florida, 1488.

9   State of Florida, 1526.

9   State of Florida.

9   State of Florida.

9   State of Florida.

10–11   "Reform School Needs Reformation," *Evening Independent,* quoting from Tampa Times, April 9, 1915, http://www.thewhitehouseboysonline.com /ARCHIVE-REFORM-SCHOOL-NEEDS-REFORMATION.html.

12   Thomas Everette Chochran, *History of Public-School Education in Florida* (Lancaster, PA: New Era, 1921), 150.

16   Board of Commissioners of State Institutions, *Learning to Live at the Florida School for Boys at Marianna* (Marianna, FL: Florida School for Boys at Marianna, Class in Printing, 1958), 3.

17–18   Antoinette Harrell, Richard Huntly, John Bonner, Johnny Lee Gaddy, and Arthur Huntley, *Dark Days of Horror at Dozier: Rapes, Murders, Beatings & Slavery* (San Bernardino, CA: Black Boys at Dozier Reform School, 2013), 119–120.

24   Johnny Lee Gaddy, *They Told Me Not to Tell: "Dozier Reform School Was a Living Hell"* (self-pub., 2015), 104.

26–27   Gaddy, 30.

28   Roger Dean Kiser, *The White House Boys: An American Tragedy* (Deerfield Beach, FL: Health Communications, 2009), 144–145.

31   Robin Gaby Fisher, *The Boys of the Dark: A Story of Betrayal and Redemption in the Deep South,* with Michael O'McCarthy and Robert Straley (New York: St. Martin's, 2010), 68.

32   Gaddy, *They Told Me.* 24.

42   Gaddy, 31.

42   Gaddy, 70.

43   Gaddy, 33.

43   Gaddy, 71.

45 Robert W. Straley, "Dozier School for Boys, Part 1: The White House Boys," interview by Dee Dee Sharp, *Aware TV Special Edition,* Pensacola State College, *WSRE,* aired November, 12, 2015, video, 6:49, http://www.pbs .org/video/aware-dozier-school-boys-part-1-white-house-boys/.

48 Harrell, Huntly, Bonner, Gaddy, and Huntley, *Dark Days,* 132.

49 Harrell, Huntly, Bonner, Gaddy, and Huntley, *Dark Days,* 141.

49 Harrell, Huntly, Bonner, Gaddy, and Huntley, *Dark Days,* 136.

51 Kiser, *White House Boys,* 37.

53 Kiser, *White House Boys,* 22–23.

54 Gaddy, *They Told Me,* 13.

55 Gaddy, 13–16.

55 Gaddy, 33.

60 Fisher, *Boys of the Dark,* 28.

66 Megan Towey, "The Search for the Dead: Victims of Alleged Abuse at Shuttered Dozier Juvenile Detention Facility Push for Justice, Part 3," *CBS,* August 12, 2013, https://www.cbsnews.com/news/the-search-for-the-dead -victims-of-alleged-abuse-at-shuttered-dozier-juvenile-detention-facility-push -for-justice/.

67 Kiser, *White House Boys,* 181.

67–68 Fisher, *Boys of the Dark,* 206.

69 John Bonner, video news story by Chris Trenkmann, "Rape, Torture, Murder Alleged at Dozier Reform School," *ABC, WFTS* Tampa Bay, August 4, 2013, 1:21, https://www.abcactionnews.com/news/rape-torture-murder-alleged-at -dozier-reform-school.

72 Florida Department of Law Enforcement, Office of Executive Investigations, "Case No. EI-73-8455, Arthur G. Dozier School for Boys, Marianna, Florida Investigative Summary," May 14, 2009, 16–18.

76–77 Richard Dean Kiser, "FDLE Investigative Report, Conclusions," Original White House Boys, accessed February 18, 2019, http://thewhitehouseboys .com/fdlereport.html.

77 Towey, "Search for the Dead."

79 United States Department of Justice, Civil Rights Division, "Investigation of the Arthur G. Dozier School for Boys and the Jackson Juvenile Offender Center, Marianna, Florida," December 1, 2011, 2.

81 Rich Phillips, "Florida Requests Exhumations at Former Boys' School," *CNN,* last modified March 12, 2013, https://www.cnn.com/2013/03/12 /justice/florida-boys-graves/.

83 "USF's Erin Kimmerle Speaks at the Dozier Site," YouTube video, 1:19, posted by Tallahassee, FL WUSF Public Media, March 28, 2013, https://www.youtube.com/watch?v=WUjp-jlgXm4.

91 Sascha Cordner, "Getting Closure over Dozier: How One Family's Story Keeps Hope Alive for Others," *WFSU*, August 8, 2014, http://news.wfsu.org/post/getting-closure-over-dozier-how-one-familys-story-keeps-hope-alive-others.

93 Erin H. Kimmerle, E. Christian Wells, Antoinette Jackson, "Summary of Findings on the Investigation into the Deaths and Burials at the Former Arthur G. Dozier School for Boys in Marianna, Florida," 15, University of South Florida, January 18, 2016, http://news.usf.edu/article/articlefiles/7173-usf-final-dozier-summary-2016.pdf.

97 Sascha Cordner, "After Final Report, Unanswered Questions Still Remain for Dozier School, Remains," *WFSU*, Tallahassee, FL, January 22, 2016, http://news.wfsu.org/post/after-final-report-unanswered-questions-still-remain-dozier-school-remains.

99 Lloyd Dunkelberger, "Legislature Apologizes for Abusive Dozier Boys School," *Orlando Sentinel,* April 26, 2017, https://www.orlandosentinel.com/news/politics/political-pulse/os-dozier-boys-apology-20170426-story.html.

99 Maya Salam, "Florida Prepares to Apologize for Horrors at Boys' School," *New York Times,* April 6, 2017, https://www.nytimes.com/2017/04/06/us/dozier-school-for-boys-florida-apology.html.

100 Mike Vasilinda, "Final Resting Place for Dozier Boys Set," *WCTV*, August 21, 2018, https://www.wctv.tv/content/news/Final-resting-place-for-Dozier-boys-set-491391671.html.

100 Ashton Williams, "'White House Boys' Tour Dozier Campus," MyPanhandle.com, April 9, 2018, https://www.mypanhandle.com/news/white-house-boys-tour-dozier-campus/1105160802.

100 Salam, "Florida Prepares to Apologize."

102 Harrell, Huntly, Bonner, Gaddy, and Huntley, *Dark Days*, 172, 173, 174.

Glossary

archaeologist: a scientist who uses the materials left behind by human activity to analyze and reconstruct the past

archives: historical records that historians collect and keep to help document the activities of a group or organization

artifacts: human-made items that when discovered and analyzed in a burial or archaeological site can help investigators interpret circumstances or relevant facts

artificial insemination: the injection of male semen into a female for purposes of reproduction by means other than sexual intercourse

biological and forensic anthropologist: a scientist with expertise in human biology, including human genetics and the human body (especially the skeletal system), who can use that knowledge to assist in legal matters and other research questions

class action lawsuit: a legal charge brought about by or representing a group of individuals who share a common grievance or complaint against a person, action, or institution

computerized facial approximation: the construction of the likely facial appearance of an unidentified person through use of computer software programs. The forensic artist typically uses the biological anthropologist's assessment of the person's sex, age, and ancestry to create the image.

cultural and historical anthropologist: a scientist who has expertise in human interactions, traditions, and sociological practices, including historical and modern customs

death certificate: a public record that lists known information about a person who has died. This information usually includes the individual's name, sex, age, race, date and time of death, cause and manner of death (natural, accident, suicide, homicide, or unknown), and where the death occurred. Depending on the county or state, other information may also be included, such as birth date, marital status, next of kin, and other data about the person's life.

deoxyribonucleic acid (DNA): a molecule found in all cells, DNA is the genetic information used within cells to direct cell activities. DNA is passed down to offspring during reproduction. Forensic scientists and others use DNA samples to try to establish biological relationships between people. They also use DNA to compare unknown biological material (bones, saliva, semen, and blood) to samples of known DNA.

electroconvulsive therapy (ECT): the use of electric shocks to the brain as a treatment for mental illness. ECT was formerly called electroshock therapy.

electroencephalography (EEG): a technique for monitoring, recording brain waves, or both, which are electrical in nature

environmental anthropologist: a scientist with expertise in the connections between humans and the natural environment, including human uses of fire, water, and raw materials. This scientist also has expertise in human relationships with other animals and with plants.

excavation: digging with mechanical or hand tools to uncover artifacts, graves, and other buried items

felony: a violent crime, such as murder and rape. Felonies can also include drug crimes and financial crimes, depending on their severity.

forensic science: the application of scientific principles and techniques to the analysis of criminal activity and other legal matters

ground-penetrating radar (GPR): a method of examining features below the surface of the earth using high-frequency electromagnetic radio waves. When radar pulses hit disturbances, such as buried items, they bounce back to a receiver that records the location and depth of the object or disturbance within the ground.

hemoglobin: oxygen-carrying, red-pigmented (red-colored) protein found in human red blood cells as well as in the blood of many other animals

industrial school: an educational institution in which students learn about manufacturing processes, such as various types of factory work that turn raw materials into useful products. These skills include learning to operate machinery to make clothing, furniture, and other household goods or to process crops, meats, and milk into commercial food products.

juvenile delinquent or offender: a young person who displays criminal tendencies, such as violent behavior or refusal to attend school. A juvenile offender may also have committed actual crimes.

misdemeanor: a minor legal offense, such as trespassing or vandalism, that is a less serious crime than a felony and for which the punishment is less severe

pathologist: a medical doctor or scientist who studies or diagnoses diseases in tissues, organs, or body systems

phenolphthalein: a chemical that when modified into a testing solution can be used to detect the presence of hemoglobin in blood. If hemoglobin is present, the test solution turns bright pink. Crime scene investigators and forensic scientists use this test solution on surfaces, clothing, and other items to see if blood may be present, even if that blood is no longer visible to the eye.

positive identification: the true identity of an individual based on scientific evidence. In forensic science, a positive identification can result from DNA testing, fingerprints, dental records, serial-numbered medical devices, and other definitive features.

presumptive identification: a tentative identity assigned to an individual based on circumstances or other clues. In forensic science, a presumptive or tentative identity is a hypothesis that requires further testing and analysis before it can become a positive identification.

reformatory school: a place where troubled young people were taught, with the intention that they improve their behavior and gain new life skills. Some reform schools were places for young offenders to serve a sentence for wrongdoing.

rehabilitate: to restore to an improved state of being. In human terms, this can be restoration of a person to better physical or mental health or a transition from harmful conduct to behavior that is more acceptable in society.

statute of limitation: a legally defined period of time beyond which the courts will no longer review a crime or other legal matter. Statutes of limitation for crimes often depend on the specifics of the offense (such as whether a weapon was used) and how quickly the crime was reported after it happened. The time period can vary considerably among states as determined by state law.

stratigraphy: the study of the relationships and layering among components and objects of the surface of the earth (rocks, minerals, and soils). It is a key part of the sciences of archaeology, paleontology, and geology.

total station surveying system: a digital, computerized system that archaeologists and others use to create a map that shows the three-dimensional locations of and relationships among objects, features, or other structures. This technology can be used at crime scenes, at archaeology sites, or for construction purposes.

Selected Bibliography

Cox, Dale. *Death at Dozier School: The Attempted Assassination of an American City.* Bascom, FL: Old Kitchen Books, 2014.

Fisher, Robin Gaby. *The Boys of the Dark: A Story of Betrayal and Redemption in the Deep South.* With Michael O'McCarthy and Robert Straley. New York: St. Martin's, 2010.

Florida Department of Law Enforcement. "Arthur G. Dozier School for Boys, Case Numbers EI-04-0005 & EI-73-8455." Office of Executive Investigations, December 18, 2012. Available at https://bloximages.newyork1.vip.townnews.com/dothaneagle.com/content/tncms/assets/v3/editorial/d/56/d5664504-67ba-50a9-bd84-c5159da75f17/55c12f6d179d5.pdf.pdf.

Gaddy, Johnny Lee. *They Told Me Not to Tell: "Dozier Reform School Was a Living Hell."* San Bernardino, CA: Johnny Lee Gaddy, 2015.

Harrell, Antoinette, Richard Huntly, John Bonner, Johnny Lee Gaddy, and Arthur Huntley. *Dark Days of Horror at Dozier: Rapes, Murders, Beatings & Slavery.* 2013.

Kimmerle, Erin H., E. Christian Wells, and Antoinette Jackson. *Report on the Investigation into the Deaths and Burials at the Former Arthur G. Dozier School for Boys in Marianna, Florida.* Tampa: Florida Institute of Forensic Anthropology & Applied Science, University of South Florida, January 2016. Available at http://mediad.publicbroadcasting.net/p/wusf/files/201601/usf-final-dozier-summary-2016.pdf.

Kiser, Roger Dean. *The White House Boys: An American Tragedy.* Deerfield Beach, FL: Health Communications, 2009.

Kushner, David. *The Bones of Marianna.* Atavist, September 2013.

United States Department of Justice, Civil Rights Division. *Investigation of the Arthur G. Dozier School for Boys and the Jackson Juvenile Offender Center, Marianna, Florida.* US Department of Justice, Civil Rights Division, December 1, 2011. https://www.justice.gov/sites/default/files/crt/legacy/2011/12/02/dozier_findltr_12-1-11.pdf.

Further Information

Books

Board of Commissioners of State Institutions. *Learning to Live at the Florida School for Boys at Marianna.* Marianna: The Florida School for Boys at Marianna, Class in Printing, 1958. Available at https://archive.org/details/learningtoliveat00flor
This booklet has been scanned into the Internet Archives and contains details about life at Dozier in the 1950s.

Burch, Jennings Michael. *They Cage the Animals at Night: The True Story of an Abandoned Child's Struggle for Emotional Survival.* New York: Berkley, 1985.
This is the story of a boy whose mother dropped him off at an orphanage, after which he spent a childhood full of abuse and neglect, passing through a series of orphanages, foster homes, and other institutions.

Dispenza, Mary. *Split: A Child, a Priest, and the Catholic Church.* Bellevue, WA: Moon Day, 2014.
This is the firsthand telling of a young girl's sexual abuse at the hands of a Catholic priest when she was just seven years old. She eventually became a Catholic nun and later was part of a successful class action lawsuit against the priest who had abused her.

Hentz, Trace L. *Stolen Generations: Lost Children of the Indian Adoption Projects.* Greenfield, MA: Blue Hand Books, 2016.
This is a collection of writings from American Indian survivors who were taken from their birth parents by the US and Canadian governments and placed into boarding schools and orphanages in the nineteenth century and into the mid-twentieth century.

Keyser, Amber J. *No More Excuses: Dismantling Rape Culture.* Minneapolis: Twenty-First Century Books, 2019.
This nonfiction title explores rape, sexual harassment, and other forms of sexual assault and abuse. It explores the #MeToo movement and other social justice movements that are working to combat discrimination and other forces that promote rape culture.

Murray, Hallie, and Ann Byers. *Living and Dying in Nazi Concentration Camps (Tales of Atrocity and Resistance: First-Person Stories of Teens in the Holocaust).* Berkeley Heights, NJ: Enslow, 2018.
This collection of survivor accounts from people who spent their teenage years abused and neglected in Nazi concentration camps during World War II is for a young adult audience.

Nichols, Pierre L. *Secrets of the Blue Door.* Albuquerque, NM: Mercury Heartlink, 2017.
This is a true story authored by a man who exposed sexual abuse and the death of a boy at a ranch for troubled youth in New Mexico.

Pelzer, Dave. *A Child Called "It."* Deerfield Beach, FL: Health Communications, 2010.

This firsthand account tells the story of a young man who was starved and beaten by an alcoholic and sadistic mother. Pelzer was finally rescued from his abusive home by a schoolteacher.

Richardson, Kim Michele. *The Unbreakable Child: A Story about Forgiving the Unforgivable.* Self-published, 2012.

This story is a firsthand account of a woman who was placed in an abusive home for orphans in rural Kentucky where she suffered emotional and physical abuse at the hand of Catholic nuns.

Wagner, Laura. *In Final Report, Experts Identify Remains at Notorious Reform School.* National Public Radio, January 21, 2016. https://www.npr.org/sections/thetwo -way/2016/01/21/463846093/in-final-report-experts-identify-remains-at -notorious-reform-school.

This piece summarizes the USF final report and contains a link to it. The story also covers the racial disparity among Dozier victims.

Whitehead, Colson. *The Nickel Boys.* New York: Doubleday, 2019.

This historical novel by the author of the award-winning novel *The Underground Railroad* tells the story of two teen boys at a reform school in Florida. The school is based on the Dozier School for Boys.

Wittenstein, Vicki Oransy. *For the Good of Mankind? The Shameful History of Human Medical Experimentation.* Minneapolis: Twenty-First Century Books, 2014.

With coverage of Nazi medical crimes against humanity, the Tuskegee Syphilis Study (1932–1972), the Henrietta Lacks biospecimen abuse story, twenty-first-century stem cell research, and more, this overview explores the history and ethics of human medical experimentation across the centuries.

Audio and Video

Allen, Greg. "Florida's Dozier School for Boys: A True Horror Story." *National Public Radio.* October 15, 2012. https://www.npr.org/2012/10/15/162941770/floridas -dozier-school-for-boys-a-true-horror-story.

This radio report provides good background information about the origins of the Dozier story and the start of the USF exhumation project.

Arkin, Daniel. "'They're Going to Find Out the Truth': Florida to Excavate Remains of Boys Who Died at Reform School." *NBC News,* August 6, 2013. https:// www.nbcnews.com/news/us-news/theyre-going-find-out-truth-florida-excavate -remains-boys-who-flna6C10863358.

This television report covers the initial authorization for and plans to exhume graves at Dozier.

"Black and White Boys at Dozier Reform School: 'Worst Nightmare.'" YouTube video, 8:05. Posted by Antoinette Harrell, July 10, 2013. https://www.youtube .com/watch?v=7OncO8OF4FE.
    This video contains numerous interviews with Dozier School survivors as well as historic images of the school.

Michot, Emily, and Candace Barbot. "The 'White House Boys': A Florida Horror Story." *Miami Herald* video, October 10, 2017. https://www.miamiherald.com /news/special-reports/florida-prisons/article177403656.html
    Narrated by Carol Marbin Miller, who broke the story about the White House Boys, this video summarizes the alleged abuses and includes old photos and video footage of the school, along with video and audio commentary from survivors.

Public Broadcasting Service. *Aware Show—Dozier School for Boys, Part 1: The White House Boys. WSRE* Pensacola, FL. Aired November 12, 2015. https://video.wsre .org/video/aware-dozier-school-boys-part-1-white-house-boys/.
    The first of a two-part TV series interviews men who were at Dozier School.

———. *Aware Show—Dozier School for Boys, Part 2: The Community Speaks Out. WSRE* Pensacola, FL. Aired November 21, 2015. https://video.wsre.org/video /aware-dozier-school-boys-part-2-community-speaks-out/.
    The second of a two-part TV series interviews community members who lived in the area around Dozier School and were involved in helping raise awareness of the story of abuse at the school.

"White House Boys 1," YouTube video, 6:52. Posted by *Jacksonville Florida Times-Union,* February 2012. https://www.youtube.com/watch?v=ztg6zBlDzb4.
    This video contains interviews with three former inmates, now adult men, of Dozier School.

"White House Boys 2," YouTube video, 3:36. Posted by *Jacksonville Florida Times-Union,* February 2012. https://www.youtube.com/watch?v=ztg6zBlDzb4.
    This video contains interviews with two former staff members and two former inmates of Dozier School.

Newspaper, Magazine, and Web Articles

Blakemore, Erin. "Archaeologists Finally Know What Happened at this Brutal Reform School." *Smithsonian.com,* January 25, 2016. https://www .smithsonianmag.com/smart-news/archaeologists-finally-know-what -happened-brutal-reform-school-180957911/.
    Coverage in the *Smithsonian Magazine* of the USF excavations at Dozier contains many useful links to further information about the project.

Bulit, David. "Arthur G. Dozier School for Boys." Abandoned Florida, September 29, 2015. https://www.abandonedfl.com/arthur-g-dozier-school-for-boys/. This photo essay with text covers the history and imagery of the now-abandoned Dozier property.

Cafe, Rebecca. "Winterbourne View: Abuse Footage Shocked Nation." *BBC News*, Occtober 26, 2012. https://www.bbc.com/news/uk-england-bristol-20084254. A BBC News web article covers the abuse of patients at a residential care facility in Bristol, England, UK. A reporter went undercover in 2011 and witnessed the severe physical and mental abuse endured by patients with learning disabilities and autism.

Emmerich, Greg. "Discovering the Truth about the Dozier School for Boys." ISHI, June 20, 2016. https://www.ishinews.com/discovering-truth-dozier-school-boys/. This story has numerous links to other media covering the Dozier School.

Farrington, Brendan. "Florida Reform School Abuse Victims Recall Horrors." *USA Today,* October 22, 2008. http://usatoday30.usatoday.com/news/nation/2008 -10-22-3487554505_x.htm. This article covers the ceremony at which the Dozier white house was sealed.

James, Susan Donaldson. "Florida Graves Reveal Reform School Horrors, Recall Witnesses and Families." *ABC News,* September 6, 2013. https://abcnews .go.com/US/florida-graves-reveal-reform-school-horrors-recall-witnesses /story?id=20172337. This article contains information about segregation at Dozier and the death of George Owen Smith, written before his remains were positively identified.

Longa, Lyda, and Tony Holt. "Remains of Boy Who Died at Dozier Reform School Sent to Daytona Sister." *Daytona Beach News-Journal.* Last modified August 12, 2016. http://www.news-journalonline.com/news/20160811/remains-of-boy-who -died-at-dozier-reform-school-sent-to-daytona-sister. This article focuses on the return of Billey Jackson to his family and contains numerous images and links to other stories about the Dozier School for Boys.

Marbin Miller, Carol. "Arthur G. Dozier School for Boys: Men Recall Abuse, Torture by Guards at Old Florida Reform School." *Miami Herald*, October 22, 2008. https://www.miamiherald.com/news/state/article214677760.html. This is the initial newspaper article by Carol Marbin Miller that originally broke the story of abuse at Dozier.

Montgomery, Ben. "Ground Truth: In Dozier's Neglected Cemetery, a Search for Lost Boys and the Reasons Why They Died." *Tampa Bay Times.* Last modified April 11, 2015. http://www.tampabay.com/news/humaninterest/ground-truth-in -doziers-neglected-cemetery-a-search-for-lost-boys-and-the/2210734. This detailed article describes the many stages of investigation into the Dozier School.

Phillips, Rich. "Reform School Guard Denies Beating Boys." *CNN*, June 16, 2009. http://www.cnn.com/2009/CRIME/06/16/florida.boys.school.lawsuit/index .html#cnnSTCText.
This online story contains information about and links to the testimony of Dozier guard Troy Tidwell during his deposition in a lawsuit brought against him by four Dozier survivors.

———. "Whatever Is below Those Crosses Is Crying Out." *CNN*, January 30, 2009. http://www.cnn.com/2009/CRIME/01/30/florida.boys.school/.
This online article covers unfolding stories of physical and sexual abuse at Dozier as they were beginning to be made public.

Salam, Maya. "Florida Prepares to Apologize for Horrors at Boys' School." *New York Times*, April 6, 2017. https://www.nytimes.com/2017/04/06/us/dozier-school-for -boys-florida-apology.html.
This account of the public apology to the men who suffered at Dozier, developed by Florida governmental representatives, contains additional links for more information.

Smith, Mark. "Untold Stories of the Notorious Ely Hospital Are Heard for the First Time in a New Exhibition." Wales Online, March 23, 2016. https://www .walesonline.co.uk/news/health/untold-stories-notorious-ely-hospital-11086371.
This article contains images and information related to Ely Hospital, an institution in Wales, United Kingdom, originally founded in 1862 as the Poor Law Industrial School for Orphan Children, which became a hospital for those with mental health issues and learning disabilities. The institution remained open for decades even after abuse was exposed in 1969.

Straley, Robert. "Straley: Dozier Atrocities Must Not Be Forgotten." *USA Today*, April 1, 2017. https://www.usatoday.com/story/opinion/2017/04/01/straley -dozier-atrocities-must-forgotten/99877102/.
This opinion piece by former inmate Robert Straley contains links to other *USA Today* stories about the Dozier School for Boys.

Towey, Megan. "The Search for the Dead: Families of Boys Who Died at Shuttered Dozier Juvenile Detention Facility Seek Answers." *CBS News*, August 8, 2013. https://www.cbsnews.com/news/the-search-for-the-dead-families-of-boys-who -died-at-shuttered-dozier-juvenile-detention-facility-seek-answers/
This is the first of a four-part series about Dozier, covering the stories of the families of former inmates Thomas Varnadoe and Owen Smith. It includes modern and historic images, video, and other links.

——— "The Search for the Dead: Former Inmates at Shuttered Dozier Juvenile Detention Facility Detail Alleged Abuse." *CBS News*, August 9, 2013. https:// www.cbsnews.com/news/the-search-for-the-dead-former-inmates-at-shuttered -dozier-juvenile-detention-facility-detail-alleged-abuse/.
The second in a four-part series discusses allegations of abuse at Dozier, including the 2007 abuse of Justin Caldwell.

———. "The Search for the Dead: Victims of Alleged Abuse at Shuttered Dozier Juvenile Detention Facility Push for Justice." *CBS News*, August 12, 2013. https://www.cbsnews.com/news/the-search-for-the-dead-victims-of-alleged-abuse-at-shuttered-dozier-juvenile-detention-facility-push-for-justice/.
The third in a four-part series covers the formation of the White House Boys and their search for legal assistance and justice.

———. "The Search for the Dead: Exhumation of Bodies Set to Begin at Shuttered Dozier Juvenile Detention Facility." *CBS News*, August 13, 2013. https://www.cbsnews.com/news/the-search-for-the-dead-exhumation-of-bodies-set-to-begin-at-shuttered-dozier-juvenile-detention-facility/.
This is the final installment in a four-part series. It discusses the investigations of the Dozier cemetery and the plans for exhumations.

University of South Florida. "Final Report for Archaeological Work and Excavation at Dozier School for Boys Released." *USF News*, January 19, 2016. http://news.usf.edu/article/templates/?a=7173&z=224&utm_source=final-dozier-report-011916&utm_medium=widget&utm_campaign=usfhomepage.
This article has numerous links to other articles, videos, and media about the work of the USF team during the Dozier School investigation.

WFTV web staff. "Survivors of Dozier School for Boys Relive Reform School Horrors as Florida Prepares for Apology." *WFTV* Orlando, FL, April 7, 2017. https://www.wftv.com/news/florida/survivors-of-dozier-school-for-boys-relive-reform-school-horrors-as-florida-prepares-apology/510320858.
This story discusses the Florida Senate Judiciary Committee's bill proposing an apology for the harm done to former students of Dozier.

Index

About the Author

Elizabeth A. Murray has been an educator and a forensic scientist for more than thirty years. Her primary teaching focus is human anatomy and forensic science. She is one of only about one hundred anthropologists currently certified as an expert by the American Board of Forensic Anthropology. Murray was the scientific consultant and on-camera personality for the miniseries *Skeleton Crew* for the National Geographic Channel and a regular cast member on the Discovery Health Channel series *Skeleton Stories*. She has written and delivered two lecture series, *Trails of Evidence: How Forensic Science Works* and *Forensic History: Crimes, Frauds, and Scandals,* produced on DVD by The Teaching Company's The Great Courses. Murray is also the author of *Forensic Identification: Putting a Name and Face on Death; Death: Corpses, Cadavers, and Other Grave Matters;* and *Overturning Wrongful Convictions: Science Serving Justice* for young adult readers.

Photo Acknowledgments

Image credits: Courtesy State Archives of Florida, pp. 4, 7, 14, 16, 20, 23, 27; National Archives (165-WW-269G-17), p. 11; Edmund D. Fountain/ZUMA Press/Newscom, pp. 30, 33, 78, 80, 85, 87; St. Petersburg Times/ZUMA Press/Newscom, p. 35; Nina Berman/NOOR/Redux, pp. 40, 48, 68; Emily Michot/Miami Herald/Tribune News Service/Getty Images, pp. 46, 58; AP Photo/Phil Coale, pp. 51, 61; Al Diaz/ Miami Herald, p. 63; Edmund D. Fountain/St. Petersburg Times/ZUMA Press, Inc./ Alamy Stock Photo, p. 70; State of Florida/Wikimedia Commons (public domain), p. 81; Sue Rhinehart/University of South Florida, p. 83; Laura Westlund/Independent Picture Service, p. 94; James Borchuck/ZUMA Press/Newscom, p. 95; Edmund D. Fountain/POOL/REUTERS/Newscom, p. 98; aPhoenixPhotographer/Shutterstock.com, (background throughout).

Cover: Courtesy of State Archives of Florida; Milan M/Shutterstock.com (design element).